C000130866

CAN THERE BE LIFE WITHOUT THE OTHER?

SOUT

'7'

Also available from Carcanet Press and the
Fundação Calouste Gulbenkian

Can There Be Life Without the Other?

Edited by António Pinto Ribeiro

CARCANET

and

FUNDAÇÃO
CALOUSTE
GULBENKIAN

First published in Great Britain in 2009 by
Carcanet Press Limited
Alliance House
Cross Street
Manchester M2 7AQ

Co-published with Fundação Calouste Gulbenkian

FUNDAÇÃO
CALOUSTE
GULBENKIAN

Copyright © Emílio Rui Vilar, António Pinto Ribeiro, Arjun Appadurai,
Dipesh Chakrabarty, Eunice de Souza, Filip De Boeck, Jorge Vala,
Karen Armstrong, Katerina Brezinova, Manuela Ribeiro Sanches, Ming Tiampo,
Mustapha Tlili, Ruy Duarte de Carvalho, Sherifa Zuhur, Jorge Sampaio 2009

The right of each contributor to be identified as the author of his or her work
has been asserted by him or her in accordance with the
Copyright, Designs and Patents Act of 1988
All rights reserved

Lawrence Durrell's translation of the poem *The City* by Constantine Cavafy
is reproduced with permission of Curtis Brown Group Ltd, London
on behalf of the Estate © Lawrence Durrell 1957

A CIP catalogue record for this book is available from the British Library
ISBN 978 1 84777 046 2

Set in Monotype Dante by XL Publishing Services, Tiverton
Printed and bound in England by SRP Ltd, Exeter

Contents

Foreword

I am not inclined to hermetist musings, but I should like to begin this brief speech of mine at the opening session of the Gulbenkian Conference, devoted to the theme of the limits and possibilities of interculturality, with some recent experiences of my own that I immediately associated with the provocative question that Professor Arjun Appadurai thought it pertinent to address to us: 'Can there be life without the Other?' I have just returned from Seville, where I attended the Ninth Meeting of the Iberian–American Forum, and during my stay there I had the opportunity to revisit the Alcázar, one of the iconic monuments of the Muslim presence in the Iberian Peninsula between the eighth and fifteenth centuries.

In 1928, some eighty years ago, during a prolonged visit to Spain, our founder, Calouste Gulbenkian, was to write the following notes about the same Alcázar in his travel diaries:

"I spent the whole afternoon in a state of rapture and reverie standing before these unforgettable architectural, decorative and fanciful riches of the *Thousand and One Nights*. Even in dreams, it is not possible to imagine anything that can rival this in its magnificence, or display such wonderful caprices of sculpture and colour. Suddenly, Seville became a sanctuary for me. In the Alcázar, we are not only faced with a paradise of Moorish art, but we find ourselves in an architectural paradise of all time..."

and he ends thus: 'everything hovers in the air for those who know how to feel it'.

It is, in fact, a magical place that perhaps also inspired King Charles V of Spain, when, together with Ferdinand Magellan, he planned there the journey for the circumnavigation of the Earth, the last of the great voyages of the first period of globalisation.

In the next issue of the *New York Review of Books*, due to come out on 6 November 2008, Professor Kwame Anthony Appiah puts his name to an article entitled 'How Muslims Made Europe', an extensive review of the book *God's Crucible: Islam and the Making of Modern Europe*, by Professor David Levering Lewis, who brings us yet another new theory in response to the recurrent question of European identity. According to this author, there were two things that made the Europeans think about themselves as a people: one was the creation by Charlemagne of the Holy Roman Empire; another was the development of the Muslim culture in the south of the Iberian Peninsula, which the Arabs called al-Andalus. Lewis's innovative thesis is not, however, based on the definition of identity through difference, but rather he claims that in the process of building the culture that the modern Europeans have inherited, the legacy of al-Andalus is, at least, as important as the legacy of the Catholic Franks. As Appiah summarises the idea: 'In borrowing from their great Other, they filled out the European Self.' Or, in other words, inclusion enriches whereas exclusion impoverishes.

I do not wish to get bogged down in historical digressions, but it seems to me that these associations enable us to sketch out a preliminary answer to the question raised by Professor Appadurai. We cannot live without the Other, because the Other is an inalienable part of ourselves. A different question to be asked, however, is how we relate to the Other, how we become aware of our cultural conditioning when we live in close proximity to the Other.

This conference can be considered yet another period of reflection in the dynamic and multidisciplinary process that the Calouste Gulbenkian Foundation has been developing for six years in the area of migrations and interculturality. Migrations are one of the priority areas for our intervention in the social world. This is a relatively recent question in Portuguese society, but nonetheless an important and complex one with diverse and multifaceted implications. It has also given rise to contradictory reactions that are frequently limiting and are also often based on received ideas and stereotypes.

The Foundation's intervention in this area is centred around three main axes: reflection and debate; concrete actions in the field; and the promotion of cultural exchanges. Thus, in a complex question such as this, it is essential to find out more, and indeed to learn more through reflection. We have therefore sought to lend our support to study and research, encouraging more work of an academic nature, debate and critical thinking.

Secondly, we have tested the concrete experience of pilot schemes that produce immediate results and advantages and are intended to create demonstration effects. A good example of this type of intervention is our project designed to support the recognition of the qualifications of immigrant doctors and nurses, which has made their social and professional integration possible. The success of this initiative was recognised by the Ministry of Health, which recently decided to support the launch of a new programme.

Thirdly and finally, we have been seeking to create a space in which the voice of immigrants can be heard. Establishing contacts with the communities and gathering together their testimonies encourages the development of a positive rhetoric about immigration and about the values of freedom and dialogue between cultures. Cultural exchanges are also, undoubtedly, an important component of any integration process. A diversified and innovative programme of arts and artistic creation was therefore prepared to enable people to discover the different dimensions (most of the time previously unknown) of the contemporary cultural reality of the immigrants who live and work in our midst.

As part of the Foundation's fiftieth anniversary commemorations, we promoted the organisation of a Cultural Forum, which we called The State of the World and which was intended to be a reflection on the current state of the world, marked by the process of globalisation and the contrasts of homogenisation and miscegenation accompanied by the sometimes radical affirmation of the right to difference, the intense circulation of people and goods, the expectation of a catastrophe, the imposition of the second virtual life, the presence of the ghost of the enemy living among us, but also the other energy coming from the emerging countries. For more than a year, the production of theories and ideas coexisted with debate and criticism; and artistic and cultural creation and practices interacted with the most diverse audiences.

This year (the European Union's year of intercultural dialogue), we launched the Gulbenkian Distance and Proximity Programme. Today, as we begin this conference, we know that many of these questions that have concerned us are again implied in the introductory texts that present this meeting, in the summaries of the speakers' papers, and in many of the themes due to be touched upon here. And yet we know that there is still a great deal to be understood, and even more remaining to be resolved. For this reason, we attempted to ensure that this conference, which forms an integral part of that programme, should have the same focus, with its title making our purpose clear: 'Can there be life without the Other? The possibilities and limits of interculturality.'

It is therefore not a question of speculating about the bankruptcy of models of inclusion or about concepts of otherness and ethnocentricity, the rights of minorities or the right to difference. The question is much more precise: knowing that interculturality is, for the time being, the most appropriate strategy for recognising that it is not possible to exclude the Other, and that it is inevitable that we should live with the Other, how are we to do this? And how are we to do this based on a clear and effective means of communication that results from our 'cultural negotiation' with the Other?

When we look at our experience, we can clearly see that there are certain moments that are better suited to decision making or when the conditions are such as to favour a more pertinent reflection. And that is very much the case today. In fact, on the one hand, we have the process of globalisation resulting in the circulation of people, goods, capital and information on an unprecedented scale and at a speed that we have never seen before, calling for rapid decisions, excluding concepts that until quite recently were fully operational, and speedily altering lifestyles. And, at the same time as all this has been going on, at this precise moment and within a very short time span, we find ourselves faced with a global financial crisis that points to a subsequent economic crisis and its inevitable social and political consequences. What effects might this crisis have for the problem that we are proposing to consider here today?

It is certainly still far too early to understand the full dimension of this crisis. But some of its effects are foreseeable. The entry of immigrants to the rich countries will immediately become more limited and some people will be forced to return to their countries of origin; humanitarian aid to populations in need will be reduced; the funding given to the NGOs working in the less favoured countries will certainly be cut – due to a lack of resources. And in the area of culture, less support will perhaps be given to research into the human and social sciences. Funding will also be withdrawn from those research centres where the sort of thinking has been developed that deals with the subjects of interest to us here today. The debate about the Other will certainly be postponed or become an even more distant prospect.

As was said earlier, we wanted this conference to focus on a specific theme, but we also wanted this theme to be dealt with from the broadest possible range of points of view and disciplines as time and space would allow. For this reason, the conference has a highly cross-disciplinary format and brings together a group of speakers originating from the most diverse cultural backgrounds and regions.

To mark the end of this conference, we will be holding the world première of twenty short films, made by an equal number of directors from the most varied cities in this world. This is also a concrete and visual, intercultural way of 'talking' with these directors, with their characters and stories, about what distinguishes and separates us, and, at the same time, about everything that we can share, which is already immense. The aim is that, by the end, what this conference will have provided will be a series of reflections and theories that, although they may not be able to save the world, may hopefully help to make it more inhabitable by and for all of us.

I wish to thank Professor Arjun Appadurai for the enormous contribution that he has provided in both the conception and organisation of this conference, and for his readiness and availability to monitor the development of the preparatory work. I also wish to tell him how eagerly we are looking forward to hearing his paper, just as I should like to express the gratitude of the Calouste Gulbenkian Foundation to all those who have agreed to take part in this conference and who will undoubtedly enrich the debate with their points of view. And, in particular, I should like to thank Jorge Sampaio, the United Nations High Representative for the Alliance of Civilisations, who will be closing the conference. Finally, I wish to congratulate António Pinto Ribeiro, who has been the coordinator of the Gulbenkian Distance and Proximity Programme. I began by evoking Seville and al-Andalus. I shall end by evoking the memory of another city that in ancient times was an example of cosmopolitanism and today seems to have been reborn with its new library and the action of the Anna Lindt Foundation: Alexandria.

At the end of the first volume of his famous Alexandria Quartet, *Justine*, Lawrence Durrell offers us the translation of a poem by Constantine Cavafy, 'The City', which most dramatically represents the emotional disturbance that is involved in all moves, ranging from the geographical to the spiritual, and from which I should like to read a few verses:

> You tell yourself: I'll be gone
> To some other land, some other sea,
> To a city lovelier far than this

Could ever have been or hoped to be –
...
There's no new land, my friend, no
New sea; for the city will follow you,
In the same streets you'll wander endlessly,
The same mental suburbs slip from youth to age,
In the same house go white at last –
The city is a cage.
No other places, always this
Your earthly landfall, and no ship exists
To take you from yourself.
...

May the city that we are now about to debate be a frank and open one.

EMÍLIO RUI VILAR
October 2008

Introduction

And now what shall become of us without any barbarians?
Those people were some kind of solution.

Many of you will immediately recognise these last two lines, as illu-
minating as they are lucid, taken from that long poem 'Waiting for
the Barbarians' (1904) by Constantine Cavafy, the poet from
Alexandria who brought Greece to Africa.

He knew then, just as we know today, that the new barbarians
– whether foreigners, immigrants or not – were and continue to
be blamed for all the world's evils: unemployment, the decline in
customs and traditions, the increased crime rates, and even the religious or political apocalypse. And yet the sciences – statistics,
sociology, history and psychology – all tell us that it is not like this:
there is a need for the barbarians and their presence is inevitable
due to the greater circulation of people in the era of globalisation
(and the population crisis faced by most western countries). This
is an era that will cause us all to cease to be either citizens or barbarians and turn us into citizens of the world. In the meantime, while
we have the privilege to live through these times of crisis, it is

imperative for us to reflect upon how impossible it is for us to live without the Other.

Of course, this 'Other' long ago ceased to be mostly a caricature of the inferior foreigner who lives among us today, essentially defined by his pronunciation or by the colour of his skin. Initially, he entered our homes through the media, in what amounted to a context of explanatory cultural anthropology. But he rapidly became just as likely to be a fellow Erasmus student, a local Chinese shopowner, a Senegalese musician playing in the city's festivities, or the Brazilian artist exhibiting in the city's gallery. And yet what appears to be an inevitability, a way of constructing democracy, is neither uncontroversial nor clear, and in fact, on the contrary, fuels conflict and rekindles racial, political and religious hatred. Ghettos exist, and so does social exclusion, communication between communities is difficult to achieve, just as the relationship between many minorities and their host majorities tends to be rife with conflict.

Where did we go wrong? What part of democracy did not work? What mistakes were and are being made in our cultural education? Some of these mistakes are known to us, for example when we reflect upon their dismal failure, as in the case of the multiculturalism that has become associated with the perspective of a static cohabitation of groups, or the rigidity of the legislation governing social contracts in the nation states. We are now beginning to try to understand others, namely when we know that, thanks to democracy, 'we', who until quite recently were the hosts of the barbarians, have now realised that our problem has variables that require complex solutions. It is worth insisting on this idea of 'we' as representing those who, after once being colonising countries or communities, have developed processes for understanding the Other, for getting to know him, for negotiating with him. We Europeans, as citizens of colonising countries, which continued to be so until very late on (1975), can include ourselves in this western process of recognising the Other in his totality: economically, as a citizen, politically and artistically.

Two years ago, in this very same room, we were given the chance to listen to a memorable concert performed by Buraka Som

Sistema, an activity that formed part of the cultural programme of the Gulbenkian Immigration Forum, which sought to give greater visibility to citizens living in Portugal who originated from other cultural regions. And let it not be said that this western process of improving our knowledge of the Other is the result of more or less collective feelings of guilt. If this alone were the reason, the results would be a complete failure. In fact, and particularly in the case of intellectual forums debating questions of a political or social nature, it was because the Others had conquered for themselves this place of public discussion, through their hard and painstaking work of study and their ceaseless demands, that such a thing happened. May I remind you that it was in 1964, at the University of Birmingham, that the Centre for Contemporary Cultural Studies was created, the result of many studies that had been initiated at the beginning of the last century about the Others of that time: the cultural production of the working class (to use the terminology of that time), mass culture, popular cultural practices, the media, cinema, jazz. It was the beginning of the 1960s. And if there are any pioneers who should be evoked here, they are, most certainly, Richard Hogarth (1918) and Stuart Hall (1932). It is to them that we owe the creation of Cultural Studies, a discipline that rapidly crossed over the Atlantic Ocean to be warmly received at American universities, giving rise to new areas of study that were full of revolutionary energy. Some of these areas are, however, no longer recognised today under the umbrella of the selfsame discipline that originally founded them.

For four decades, therefore, these questions about the Other have been worked upon by many illustrious intellectuals and artists, and we have recently had the privilege of listening to and reading some of them. Today is yet another day when we are privileged to have among us, opening this conference, Professor Arjun Appadurai. I myself was the first to benefit from this privilege, because during the course of a whole year I have had the opportunity to be able to talk with Professor Appadurai by phone or email about the most important themes that have brought us together here, as well as to read articles and books that he has written, and to share with him the criteria for choosing the illustrious speakers who have been invited to participate in this conference.

Professor Appadurai was born in Bombay. He was educated at St Xavier's High School and took a first degree at Elphinstone College, embarking thereafter on an impressive academic career in the USA, culminating in the award of a PhD at the University of Chicago, where he also worked as a lecturer. He has lectured in many other notable subjects at American universities and is a visiting professor at universities in South America and India. Professor Appadurai is, to some extent, an activist because of the way in which he has become involved in humanitarian projects promoted by UNESCO, WIDER (World Institute for Development Economics Research) and the National Science Foundation, among others. Most recently, he has been leading PUKAR (Partners for Urban Knowledge Action and Research) in Mumbai, a long-term project about culture, conflict and social crisis, which is designed to study the relationship between ethnic violence, housing, poverty and the media.

He is a prolific author, who has published hundreds of articles and books that are considered fundamental references for studying the contemporary world. I am referring, among many other editions, co-editions and anthologies, to *Worship and Conflict Under Colonial Rule: A South Indian Case* (1981), *Gender, Genre and Power in South Asian Expressive Traditions* (1991, co-edited with M. Mills and F. Korom), *Modernity at Large: Cultural Dimensions of Globalization* (1996), and *Fear of Small Numbers: An Essay on the Geography of Anger* (2002). He was also one of the founders of a review that is considered essential reading, a vanguard publication in the field of Cultural Studies, *Public Culture*. It would be inappropriate, to say the least, to continue with this long list of the body of work produced by our illustrious guest.

I cannot, however, fail to present you with three of the questions that, in my view, are the most original and pertinent in the work of Professor Appadurai, and which are directly related to the theme of this conference.

The first of these questions has to do with the relationship between the media and immigration. For Professor Appadurai (who is positioned in the area of cultural anthropology), globalisation and the consequent infinite and permanent circulation of images, together with the parallel circulation of immigrants, have meant that the image of the latter, on the one hand, has radically altered. On the other hand, the notions of identity, locality and imagination have also changed, giving rise to a simultaneous movement: 'moving images meet mobile audiences'. This, in turn, has led to the appearance of hybrid identities, ever-changing localities and collective imaginations without any strict territorial referents. It should also be noted that, for better or worse, it is the media that is mainly responsible for creating our archives on immigration (*Modernity at Large*, 1996).

A second question is related to an original conceptual architecture that explains the work of the collective imagination – a theme developed in many texts by Professor Appadurai – and which, in very brief terms, translates into the explanation of imagined worlds. It has to do with relating ethno-landscapes (the landscapes of the people who constitute the world in movement – tourists, immigrants, refugees...) with techno-landscapes (the landscapes constructed by the technologies that are rapidly spreading across all borders), financial landscapes (the strange and mysterious landscape of the capital flows taking place on a global scale), media landscapes (the result of the electronic spread of the production and dissemination of information to spectators from all over the world) and ideological landscapes (compositions of images originating from the field of politics, produced by the state's ideological instruments, or, contrary to movements that are geared towards the taking of power, with which we associate terms such as freedom, prosperity, rights, sovereignty, representation, etc.).

The third question that I present to you is taken from an article by Professor Appadurai published in volume 19 of *Public Culture*, under the title of 'Hope and Democracy', in which, according to his observation, despite the fact that democracy requires a vision for the future, it has not been possible to reconcile the political promise that is made with hope. It seems that both values, such as liberty, equality and fraternity, and rules, such as those of participation, for example, are used more as ideological arguments for the seizure of power – this was how it was with the utopian regimes of the twentieth century – than as the politics of hope. And in Professor Appadurai's view, this politics of hope needs to be inserted within a logic of transnational movements, with greater imagination and greater aspiration.

I beg Professor Appadurai to forgive me if, in my speech, there has been an excessive amount of interpretation, but I wished, above all, to present him to those who have not yet had the pleasure of reading and studying his work. I am grateful to him for the conversations that we have had and for his presence here today. Just as I am equally grateful to Jorge Sampaio for his contributions to the session about the religious questions that have been included in this conference. And, finally, I also wish to express my gratitude to all the illustrious speakers who agreed to share their ideas, theories, problems and pictures with us, just as I am also grateful to the artist Yonamine, to whom we owe the general picture that has been used to promote this conference.

When we began this Gulbenkian Distance and Proximity Programme, I remember writing: 'There will only be a more peaceful future for humanity if interculturality is possible', and I added that we should not misunderstand the place for the resolution of the various problems that interculturality presupposes. We are in a place of study, reflection and theoretical production, where a fundamental role is to be played by all the participants in this conference, in their vast majority typical personalities of the twenty-first century, for they are all citizens of the diaspora, of the various diasporas. From them, we expect to receive a contribution towards a more peaceful future for humanity.

ANTÓNIO PINTO RIBEIRO

Notes on Contributors

Emílio Rui Vilar

Emílio Rui Vilar was born in Oporto on 17 May 1939. He graduated in law from Coimbra University in 1961 and has been President of the Board of Trustees of the Calouste Gulbenkian Foundation since May 2002.

Emílio Rui Vilar is also President of the Portuguese Foundation Centre and Chairman of the European Foundation Centre. Since 1996, he has served as Chairman of the Audit Commission of the Bank of Portugal.

He served as Secretary of State for External Trade and Tourism (1974), Minister of the Economy (1974–75) and Minister of Transport and Communications (1976–78). In addition, he has served as Deputy Governor of the Bank of Portugal (1975–84); Director General of the European Community Commission (1986–89); General Commissioner of Europalia Portugal (1989–92); Chairman and CEO, Caixa Geral de Depósitos (National Savings Bank) (1989–95).

António Pinto Ribeiro

António Pinto Ribeiro was born in Lisbon in 1956. He graduated in Philosophy at the Lisbon Classic University (1981) and got a Masters degree in Communication Sciences at the Lisbon Universidade Nova (1995). Currently he is preparing his PhD, focusing on the subject of 'Conditions for artistic reception in the postcolonial time'. He is a Lecturing Professor at several universities and was the Coordinating Professor of the postgraduate course in Management of Cultural Activities at the Lisbon Institute of Social Sciences and Management (Instituto Ciências Sociais e das Empresas). In parallel, he collaborates regularly with magazines that specialise in aesthetics, theories of arts and cultures and cultural programming. He is the author of several publications. He was Culturgest's (Cultural Centre in Lisbon) Artistic Director between 1993 and 2004. He is currently a consultant at the Calouste Gulbenkian Foundation in Lisbon where he was Chief Curator of the State of the World cultural forum, Chief Coordinator of the Creativity and Artistic Creation Programme and Coordinator of the Distance and Proximity Gulbenkian Programme.

Arjun Appadurai

Arjun Appadurai is Goddard Professor of Media, Culture and Communication at New York University and Senior Research Fellow at the Max Planck Institute for the Study of Religious and Ethnic Diversity, Göttingen (Germany).

Arjun Appadurai was born and educated in Mumbai. He graduated from St Xavier's High School and earned his Intermediate Arts degree from Elphinstone College before coming to the United States. He earned his BA from Brandeis University in 1970, and his MA (1973) and PhD (1976) from the University of Chicago. Arjun Appadurai serves as Senior Advisor for Global Initiatives at The New School in New York City, where he also holds a Distinguished Professorship as the John Dewey Professor in the Social Sciences. Until recently, Arjun Appadurai was the Provost and Senior Vice-President for Academic Affairs at The New School. He has authored numerous books and scholarly articles including *Fear of*

Small Numbers: An Essay on the Geography of Anger (Duke University Press, 2006) and *Modernity at Large: Cultural Dimensions of Globalization* (University of Minnesota Press, 1996; Oxford University Press, Delhi, 1997). His previous scholarly publications have covered such topics as religion, cuisine, agriculture and mass culture in India. He is one of the founding editors, along with Carol A. Breckenridge, of the journal *Public Culture* and was the founding Director of the Chicago Humanities Institute at the University of Chicago (1992—98). He is one of the founders of the Interdisciplinary Network on Globalisation, a consortium of institutions in various parts of the world devoted to the study of global politics and culture.

Dipesh Chakrabarty

Dipesh Chakrabarty is the Lawrence A. Kimpton Distinguished Service Professor in History, South Asian Languages and Civilisations and the College at the University of Chicago. He is a founding member of the editorial collective of *Subaltern Studies*, a co-editor of *Critical Inquiry*, and a founding editor of the journal *Postcolonial Studies*. He has also served on the editorial boards of the American *Historical Review* and *Public Culture*. Professor Chakrabarty is a Fellow of the American Academy of Arts and Sciences and an Honorary Fellow of the Australian Academy of the Humanities.

Eunice de Souza

Eunice de Souza retired as Head of the Department of English, St Xavier's College, University of Bombay after thirty-one years of teaching. She has published four books of poetry, *Fix* (1979), *Women in Dutch Painting* (1988), *Ways of Belonging: Selected Poems* (1990) and *New and Selected Poems* (1994). A bilingual edition of *New and Selected Poems* was published in Portuguese and in English by Livros Cotovia, Lisbon in 2001. Eunice de Souza has published two novellas, *Dangerlok* (Penguin, 2001) and *Dev and Simran* (Penguin, 2003). She has also edited several anthologies of nineteenth- and early twentieth-century writing in English in India, in prose, fiction and poetry, for Oxford University Press; edited the contemporary poetry collection, *Nine Indian Women Poets* (Oxford University Press, 1997); a book of conversations with poets writing in English called *Talking Poems* (Oxford University Press, 1999); and editions of rare books for the Sahitya Akademi. She has written for children and with Melanie Silgardo edited a book of poems for them.

Filip De Boeck

As the coordinator of the Institute for Anthropological Research in Africa (IARA, formerly the Africa Research Centre), a Research Unit of the Faculty of Social Sciences, Professor Filip De Boeck (born Antwerp, 1961) is actively involved in teaching, promoting, coordinating and supervising research in and on Africa. Since 1987 he has conducted extensive field research in both rural and urban communities in the Democratic Republic of Congo (ex-Zaire). His current theoretical interests include local subjectivities of crisis, postcolonial memory, youth and the politics of culture, and the transformation of private and public space in the urban context in Africa.

Jorge Vala

Jorge Vala was awarded a PhD in Psychology from the University of Louvain; he was a Full Professor at the Higher Institute of Business and Labour Sciences (ISCTE) and Principal Researcher at the Institute of Social Sciences (ICS) at Lisbon University. He has been a Visiting Professor at several universities, including the University of Paris V, the École des hautes études en sciences sociales (EHESS) and the State University of Rio de Janeiro. He was a member of the management team of the European Association of Experimental Social Psychology and is currently National Coordinator of the European Social Survey and a member of both the Executive Committee and the Scientific Committee of the European Values Study. He is also a member of the Scientific Board of the Swiss Foundation for Research in Social Sciences (FORS) and President of the Scientific Board of ICS. He has undertaken research in the area of Social Psychology into socio-cognitive processes, namely in the field of social representations and social identities. The projects that he is currently working on link these processes to the study of racism, social justice and the validation of everyday knowledge. His research projects have been funded by the Portuguese Foundation for Science and Technology, the Calouste Gulbenkian Foundation and the European Science Foundation.

Karen Armstrong

Karen Armstrong is one of the most provocative, original thinkers on the role of religion in the modern world. Armstrong is a former Roman Catholic nun who left a British convent to pursue a degree in modern literature at Oxford. In 1982 she wrote a book about her seven years in the convent, *Through the Narrow Gate*, that challenged Catholics worldwide; her more recent book, *The Spiral Staircase* (2004), discusses her subsequent spiritual awakening after leaving the convent, when she began to develop her iconoclastic take on the great monotheistic religions. She has written more than twenty books around the ideas of what Islam, Judaism and Christianity have in common, and around their effect on world events, including the magisterial *A History of God* (1993) and *Holy War: The Crusades and Their Impact on Today's World* (1988). Her latest book is *The Bible: A Biography* (2007). Her meditations on personal faith and religion (she calls herself a freelance monotheist) spark discussion — especially her take on fundamentalism, which she sees in a historical context, as an outgrowth of modern culture.

Katerina Brezinova

Katerina Brezinova is a historian and anthropologist educated at universities in the Czech Republic, the USA, Spain, Mexico and Great Britain. She is a Researcher at the Institute of Latin American Studies at Charles University in Prague, and she has worked as a visiting scholar at the Universities of Carlos III de Madrid, Spain, Washington University in Saint Louis, USA, and Colegio de Mexico, Mexico. Her work has been concerned with the politics of identity, multiculturalism and migration as reflected through culture and arts, with a special focus on the regions of Latin America, Central and Eastern Europe, and Russia. Her award-winning PhD thesis on the political iconography of the Chicano Movement in the USA is to be published by Charles University

Press. As an academic, columnist and an NGO activist, her interests have always combined research and practice. She is a Founding Director of the Multicultural Center Prague (www.mkc.cz), a think tank dedicated since the late 1990s to applied social research in an increasingly culturally diverse region of Central and Eastern Europe. She is currently serving as member of the Board of Directors of the European Cultural Foundation (www.eurocult. org), dedicated to enhancing the role of culture and the arts in the context of multicultural European societies. She regularly collaborates with diverse EU institutions in the capacity of a consultant both within the EU and in non-industrialised countries. She currently lives in São Paulo, Brazil.

Manuela Ribeiro Sanches

Manuela Ribeiro Sanches is Assistant Professor at the Faculty of Letters, University of Lisbon. She is also a Researcher at the Centre for Comparative Studies at the same institution, where she coordinates the project Dislocating Europe: Postcolonial Perspectives in Literary, Anthropological and Historical Studies. She has recently edited *'Portugal não é um país pequeno'. Contar a Império na pós-colonialidade* (Cotovia, 2006); *Deslocalizar a 'Europa'. Antropologia, arte, literatura e história na pós-colonialidade* (Cotovia, 2005); and with Carlos Branco Mendes and João Ferreira Duarte, *Connecting Peoples. Identidades Disciplinares e Transculturais/ Transcultural and Disciplinary Identities* (Colibri, 2004).

Ming Tiampo

Ming Tiampo is Assistant Professor of Art History at Carleton University in Ottawa, Canada. Her current book project, *Gutai: Decentering Modernism* (University of Chicago Press, forthcoming 2010), uses Gutai's transnational activities as a case study to suggest new ways of framing modernism. Claiming a place for Gutai in the history of modernism, this book explores how it may be reconsidered both for and from the periphery, contributing to the theorisation of modernism beyond the Euro-American context. She has published and lectured in Austria, Canada, France, Germany, Japan, the United Kingdom and the United States. Her previous projects include the AICA award-winning exhibition, *Electrifying Art: Atsuko Tanaka 1954–1968* (2004–5; Grey Art Gallery, New York and Belkin Art Gallery, Vancouver). She is a founding member of the Carleton Centre for Transnational Analysis and an associate member of the Berlin Institute for Cultural Inquiry.

Mustapha Tlili

Sorbonne-educated, Mustapha Tlili is the Founder and Director of the Centre for Dialogues, a Research Scholar at New York University and Senior Fellow at its Remarque Institute. Previously, Professor Tlili taught at Columbia University's School of International and Public Affairs and was a Senior Fellow at the World Policy Institute of New School University. He is a former senior UN official, having served as Director for Communications Policy in the United Nations Department of Public Information, Director of the UN Information Centre for France, located in Paris, and Chief of the Namibia, Anti-apartheid, Palestine and Decolonisation programmes in the same department. An established novelist, Mustapha Tlili is a knight of the French Order of Arts and Letters. He is also a member of Human Rights Watch's Advisory Committee for the Middle East and North Africa.

Ruy Duarte de Carvalho

Ruy Duarte de Carvalho was born in 1941, in Portugal, and was naturalised Angolan in 1975 when Angolan citizenship came into being. From 1975 to 1981, he made films for the Angolan television station and film institute. In 1982, he obtained a diploma from the Ecole des Hautes Etudes en Sciences Sociales with a film, *Nelisita*, later receiving a PhD in Social Anthropology and Ethnology in 1986. From 1987 onwards, he taught Social Anthropology at the Universities of Luanda in Angola, São Paulo in Brazil and Coimbra in Portugal, while also conducting research into the pastoral and agropastoral societies of south-west Angola and north-west Namibia in particular.

He has published about twenty books of poetry, fiction, narratives and essays. He began his poetic works with *Chão de Oferta*

(1972), continuing with, among other books, *Observação directa* (2000) and, more recently, with *Lavra – poesia reunida 1970/2000* (2005). His published works of fiction include *Como se o mundo não tivesse leste* (1977), *Os papéis do Inglês* (2000), *Paisagens propícias* (2005) and *Desmedida. Luanda, São Paulo, São Francisco e Volta. Crónicas do Brasil* (2006). He is also the author of *Vou lá visitar pastores* (1999), a vast fresco about the Kuvale, a pastoral society from south-west Angola, and two books of essays entitled *Actas da Maianga. Dizer da(s) guerra(s) em Angola* (2003) and *A câmara, a escrita e a coisa dita... Fitas, textos e palestras* (2008).

Sherifa Zuhur

Sherifa Zuhur is the Executive Director of the Institute of Middle Eastern and Islamic Studies. She was Research Professor of Islamic and Regional Studies at the Strategic Studies Institute, US Army War College from 2004–2009. She has lectured and held faculty positions in three countries, including Massachusetts Institute of Technology, the University of California, Berkeley, and the American University in Cairo. Dr Zuhur's initial research focus was on Islamist movements in Egypt. She published additionally on women's issues and the arts in the Middle East, including a biography of the popular singer Asmahan. After joining US government service, she published a series of studies on Islamist influences in the Middle East and their security implications from Iraq to Saudi Arabia to Egypt to the West Bank and Gaza. As part of her independent research she has contributed to various international groups working on Muslim approaches to defusing violent extremism, and also on changes needed to address violence against women in the Middle East.

Jorge Sampaio

Jorge Sampaio was born in Lisbon in 1939. In 1961 he graduated in Law from the University of Lisbon, after which he took up a legal career. He became a member of the board of the Law Association, playing an important role in the defence of political prisoners. From 1979 to 1984 he was a member of the European Human Rights Commission of the Council of Europe where he played an important role in defending fundamental rights and in contributing to a more dynamic implementation of the principles contained in the European Convention on Human Rights. In 1989 he was elected Secretary General of the Socialist Party, a position he held until 1991. He was the Mayor of Lisbon between 1989 and 1995, and between 1996 and 2006 was the President of the Republic of Portugal. In May 2006 he was appointed by Kofi Annan as the UN Secretary General's Special Envoy to Stop TB and in April 2007 was appointed by Ban Ki-moon, UN Secretary General, as UN High Representative for the Alliance of Civilizations.

Dialogue, Risk and Conviviality

ARJUN APPADURAI

I will make a simple argument here about the nature of dialogue. No one can enter into dialogue without taking serious risks. This view is opposed to the commonsense view of dialogue as casual, quotidian, even secondary to the real workings of power and wealth. If we can agree that dialogue is always a risky affair, we can ask ourselves what risks are involved and why it is worthwhile, even compulsory, to take these risks today. I am mainly concerned with dialogue between societies or organised social groupings, such as nations, religions, political movements and parties, and interest groups. Still, it is worth noting that dialogue begins as an idea of exchange between persons. When I discuss the risks of dialogue today, I shall mainly have cultures and civilisations in mind, but I believe these risks are present regardless of the level at which dialogue may take place.

The Risks of Dialogue

The first risk of dialogue is that the other party may not understand what you mean. The risk of misunderstanding is inherent to all human communication, and we have evolved many ways to reduce these risks. We try to choose our words and actions carefully, we pay attention to language and translation, we try to imagine the mental assumptions of the other party, and we try to be as intersubjective as possible and to find the best ways to cross the boundaries between the speaker and the listener. Needless to say, when we conduct dialogue in earnest, we also try to listen with the same mental approach, so as to minimise the risks of misunderstanding or miscommunication.

The second risk of dialogue is exactly the opposite, and that is the risk that we may in fact be understood clearly. This paradox is partly based on the worry that the other party may see through our surface expressions and understand motives or intentions which we prefer to conceal. That is always a hazard in the era of the epistemology of suspicion, coming out of Marx, Nietzsche and Freud. But the deeper risk of being fully understood is the risk that the other party will actually see our deepest convictions, our foundational opinions and even our doubts. The reason why this is a risk is that dialogue is not about everything. To be effective, dialogue must be to some extent about shared ground, selective agreement and provisional consensus. When foundational convictions come on to the table, the improvisational element of dialogue is endangered and the stakes become impossibly high, since basic convictions have to be made commensurable. One major example of this risk is the current dialogue between the Islamic world and the Christian European world, in which dialogue too quickly moves to doctrinal and ethical foundations, without paying attention to more specific and limited arenas. A struggle over headscarves in schools need not become a struggle over competing views of human universality. It can remain a problem of public conduct or etiquette. So when we undertake dialogue, we must take care not to demand too much understanding or to offer too much of our deepest convictions. I am aware that this sounds like a suggestion that we must be hypocritical or cynical. In fact, I am suggesting prudence and limited agreement.

So let me make an interim conclusion and suggest that when we undertake dialogue, an even greater risk than the risk of misunderstanding is the risk of excess understanding. Let us probe this argument a little more fully. Complete, full and precise mutual understanding is an impossible standard, in any case, given the challenges of culture, language and history that divide individuals and communities. But complete understanding, at the level of primary ethical, religious or political convictions, carries yet another danger with it. That danger is the urge to eliminate basic differences altogether. For if we wish to establish common ground at the level of basic convictions, somebody's basic convictions must change, and this usually means that one party's deepest convictions become the measure of common ground. This is the way in which false universalisms can erase true differences. So dialogue must always involve a decision about how far to demand negotiation about fundamentals. In this sense, all dialogue is a form of negotiation and negotiation cannot be based on complete mutual understanding or a total consensus across any sort of boundary of difference.

The Importance of Internal Debates

There is yet another risk associated with dialogue and that is the relationship of dialogue to internal differences on each side of the dialogue. All individuals have inner doubts, differences and divisions within themselves, as for example between short- and long-term goals, higher and lesser motives, conscious and unconscious interests and so on. When we move up the scale to groups, communities, civilisations and other large social formations, we have in addition the internal differences between the old and the young, the elite and the common people, between the court and the street, between men and women, to name only the simplest categories of internal division. In the age of globalisation, these internal differences are further exacerbated by the movement of migrants to new locations, the different identity anxieties of old and young among migrant populations, the nature of mass media and electronic communication which allows intensely local and highly remote attachments to be co-present and mutually formative.

As far as the risks of dialogue are concerned, the central problem of internal differences is that there can be no negotiation with the other without a parallel negotiation with the self. In the world of politics, religion and nationalism, such internal negotiations take place under special circumstances which make it hard for anyone to speak confidently on behalf of others without the risk of challenge. The problem of representation by any leader or organised voice that purports to speak on behalf of any collective entity is that challenge is always possible. This sort of challenge has its general source in the gradual spread of ideas about freedom and expression that have been growing in popularity ever since the great revolutions of the eighteenth century. It has become especially strong during the last fifteen years or so, after the end of the Cold War, when ideas about market freedom and political freedom became so deeply connected. But there is yet another special reason for the difficulty of representing whole communities, civilisations or religious groups by any sort of leadership. With the creation of the United Nations Charter of Human Rights, there has been a sharp increase in the global awareness of the right to speak, to be protected, to be treated with dignity and to be granted a voice in public life for all people, regardless of their citizenship rights. Combined with the growth of electronic communication and the ideologies of participatory democracy, the spread of the ideology of human rights has meant that no person or group – women, prisoners, children, refugees, the disabled, migrants – can be treated as people who can be spoken for without their consent.

The conclusion I draw from this discussion of internal differences is that it is risky, indeed impossible, for any representative voice to speak with authority on behalf of a culture, a religion, a nation, a movement or a civilisation. Here again, the solution is to move away from the tendency to speak in totalising terms of whole societies, traditions or civilisations as if they contain no 'essentially contestable concepts'. All great religions have sceptics, doubters, dissidents and even heretics. Sometimes they are ignored, sometimes they are burnt at the stake, and sometimes, as in the case of Martin Luther King, they become founders of great religious traditions in their own right. Indeed the test of a civilisation or a great tradition may well be seen as its capacity to incite dissent, inspire debate and generate internal differences on matters of fundamental importance. Thus the risk of dialogue, from this point of view, is that it requires a tricky calculus about bringing internal debate into the dialogue with the Other. If you bring in too much internal debate, your position looks weak, illegitimate and perhaps incoherent. If you bring in too little, you look authoritarian, arrogant or simply incredible. In this regard, the risk of true dialogue is a double risk or a risk of falling into the Scylla of incoherence or the Charybdis of authoritarianism.

In contemporary Europe, it is evident that these risks are both real. Islam is too often represented as monolithic, as not having room for dissent, debate or difference. On the other hand, opponents of Islamic fundamentalism often deny the deep divisions underneath the liberal consensus: between those who are for or against the European Union; between those who come out of Catholic, Protestant or Jewish traditions; between those who have become thoroughly secularised and those who have not; between those who have come to embrace the religion of the market and those who have not; between votaries of fast and slow food; and between supporters and opponents of the welfare state. The real challenge is to choose among all these debates and decide which ones are appropriate to bring into a true dialogue. The risk is that we can make the wrong choices and end up negotiating over true foundations (which are almost always immune to real negotiation) and superficial conventions, in which common ground is not really deep or consequential.

Thus, if we wish to move away from the misleading and dangerous idea of a 'clash of civilisations', especially where Islam is concerned, it is important to recognise that all dialogue is risky and that no great tradition or ideology is lacking in internal debates. The challenge becomes how to conduct dialogue about the relevant differences, not about any difference or all differences. After all, we value diversity. How can there be diversity without difference?

If we recognise that the purpose of dialogue is not to eliminate diversity of opinion about differences, then how do we move forward in intercultural dialogue? How do we avoid the idea of a 'clash of civilisations', which amounts to a denial of the possibility of dialogue? This is of course not a question with a simple answer, but a starting point is to devote real thought to the question of the link between internal and external debates. Some internal debates are entirely internal and have little bearing on external negotiations. Other internal debates are so deep and dramatic that they cannot be brought to any sort of outside negotiation. But there is a middle ground, a set of internal debates which have a genuine but limited link to external dialogues. These are the debates which we need to identify and use to build the platform for common ground. Let us take a few examples.

If you consider the current debates between thinkers from the Islamic world and thinkers from other traditions, whether religious or political, one example of a link between external and internal debates is the subject of the obligations of any community to those who are weaker or poorer within it. This subject brings together ideas about justice, welfare, equity and philanthropy. It could be a crucial link between internal debates with Muslim communities about these subjects and external debates in European parliaments, state organisations and the public sphere. A second example concerns the relationship between Church and State in various Western democracies. This is an area where there are deep differences between internal debates in the United States and in various European countries. Bringing the internal debates in this area into the space of negotiation across the Atlantic could reveal richer grounds for trans-Atlantic dialogue than those which currently exist. Another example of an area where internal and external debates can come together concerns the issue of violence and non-violence. Among those who consider themselves to be Hindus in India today, there is a sharp difference between, on the one hand, those who still see themselves as descendants of Mahatma Gandhi, and see non-violence as a fundamental principle of moral and political life, and on the other hand, the many Hindu nationalists who have taken up a very militant approach and have directed a new kind of violent mobilisation against Muslims in

India. These internal debates among Hindu Indians have direct relevance to their approach to nuclear power, peace and the question of Kashmir. Yet they are rarely debated in a focused manner in which internal and external dimensions of the ethics of non-violence are brought together. The following section examines two examples from India which show us the complexities of risk, dialogue and negotiation, one at a high civilisational level, involving the ideas of Mahatma Gandhi, and the other involving a completely different level of social life, found in the slums of Mumbai.

Two Indian Examples of Internal Debates

Mahatma Gandhi's story invited us to connect asceticism, abnegation, abstinence and refusal as forms of political action. Gandhi was the modern world's first and greatest refusenik but his refusal took its meaning from a particular way of mobilising the inner link between asceticism, violence and non-violence in the Indic world. The best context in which to examine this inner link is to look once again at the ways in which Gandhi made civil disobedience a major part of his politics.

Civil disobedience has been argued by some to be the major political innovation which we owe to Gandhi, at least insofar as large-scale resistance to imperial or colonial rule is concerned. It is certainly that part of the Gandhian heritage which is most vital to later figures such as Martin Luther King and Nelson Mandela. There is a large technical literature on the history of Gandhian civil disobedience, focused on major events such as the Salt March, the push to refuse the use of British textiles and the refusal to accept other British legal impositions. The story of civil disobedience, as evolved in India by Gandhi, has many dimensions including the positive actions entailed by various refusals, actions such as the collection and processing of salt by Gandhi and his *satyagrahis*, the active production of *khadi* cloth as a form of daily practice and economic resistance, and the general push to economic self-reliance (*swadeshi*). Nevertheless, refusal is the first principle of civil disobedience (with its roots in Thoreau and the abolitionist movement of the nineteenth century in the United States). In India, and especially for Gandhi, there is a deep connection between refusal, abstinence and the avoidance of luxury. In other words, Gandhian civil disobedience is shot through with an ascetic ethics, which connects with other forms of abstinence and abnegation (such as fasting, celibacy and other personal practices). Each of these elements was woven by Gandhi into a larger politics of refusal, which erected personal and bodily *askesis* as an answer to the ethics of civil law.

Political refusal, in this Gandhian ethos, was intimately connected with the politics of the body and the morality of avoidance, abnegation and abstention. The idea of the boycott and the *hartal* capture the political end of this ethos as fasting captures its bodily pole. Both ends are underpinned by an ethics of abstention and an ideology of sacrifice, in the double sense of severance and offering. In the public actions of civil disobedience we see an abstemious, minimalist and parsimonious echo of the royal sacrifice and of the history of the warrior ascetic, in which abstention becomes a weapon of positive action and of militant collective mobilisation, in this case against British armed forces and the British legal order.

We are now in a better position to answer the question of what sort of action is involved in non-violence. No doubt, non-violence is a particular form of abstinence and of asceticism. But since it is also part of a larger politics of refusal and of sacrifice, it also takes its meaning from the field of violence in two distinct ways. The first, most dramatically captured in the images and reports of the waves of *satyagrahis* walking towards the British troops in the Salt March, to fall down like ninepins with their skulls bashed and their bones broken, reminds us that the active work of non-violence is to invite the forces of violence to declare and enact themselves and to manifest themselves practically, rather than as threats or deterrents. The second way in which non-violence takes its meaning from the world of violence is through the more complex genealogy I have tried to describe, which is more Indic in its form, and looks back through the traditions of warrior asceticism to the violence of the royal sacrifice as the supreme form of political performative. Gandhi's practices of non-violence thus derived their best energies from ideas of militant action which did not simply oppose love to violence but also opposed an earlier idea of militant asceticism to the imperial forms of organised and legalised police violence. The latter, a completely legalised form of coercive violence, could not have been better designed to fail in the face of the violence of the militant ascetic, the harsh discipline of abstention, that Gandhi put at the core of his own understanding of how to generate an unstoppable force through the practices of refusal.

So, non-violence can start something new in the world, and it is certainly not right to view it as the refusal of action, or as quietist in any form. But it is also important to see that the Gandhian version of the ethics of refusal also drew its force from another ethics of violence and power, associated originally with the royal sacrifice in India, and subsequently with militant asceticism. This sort of refusal needs to be handled with care, since it can and indeed has become far too available to the politics of saffron and the vulgarisation of the trident in contemporary India. This example shows us that Gandhi's idea of non-violence, far from being a simple and unambiguous idea, is the product of a complex internal negotiation between two traditions of refusal and sacrifice, which contain rather different ideas about violence, and are both *within* the Hindu tradition.

My second example also comes from India. It concerns the ways in which a very poor population of slum-dwellers in Mumbai address their own internal differences by crossing the boundaries of language, class, ethnicity and gender within their own world in Mumbai. They do so without the benefits of 'high cosmopolitanism', the cosmopolitanism of travel, literacy, philosophical reflection and deliberate self-cultivation. This is what we might call 'compulsory cosmopolitanism', negotiation across cultural boundaries without which their very existence would be at risk.

The cultural strategies of the urban poor in Mumbai involve many activist and civil society organisations. I have worked closely with a group of three organisations in Mumbai, who are part of a worldwide network of urban housing activists called the

Slum/Shackdwellers International. In India, they have mobilised themselves by organising themselves into federations, primarily through the work of the National Slum Dwellers Federation (NSDF); by building on the street experiences of the women who formed an organisation called Mahila Milan in the aftermath of their earlier struggles as sex-workers in the variety of neighbourhoods that fan out from Bombay Central, one of Mumbai's two major railways stations; and by taking advantage of the middle-class resources of the women who built up an NGO based in Mumbai known as SPARC (Society for the Protection of Area Resource Centres).

Today, in 2008, the poor women and men of Mahila Milan and NSDF have come a long way from their beginnings as self-organising urban activists struggling to gain secure housing, minimum civil rights and minimum protection from the depredations of police, criminals and the municipal authorities in Mumbai. They have learned to speak directly to banks, engineers, architects, developers, politicians, academics and international celebrities. They have learned to document, survey, monitor and regulate their own communities, through techniques of surveying, enumeration and mutual information. They have evolved sophisticated forms for articulating their own savings circles and assets with official and quasi-official banking and credit institutions. They have become the principals in a major construction company (an independent private company called NIRMAAN), through which they handle capital, loans, planning and execution of building projects centred on housing and sanitation in Mumbai and in many other Indian cities. They have vastly improved their capacity to deliver built infrastructure up to the standards of municipal and private lending authorities and have been asked by state and federal authorities to extend their experiences and strategies to cities in India which have been struggling with housing and infrastructure for the poor for decades without success. They have learned to deal with the constant movement and transfers of civil servants working for city and state agencies whose support they have learned to cultivate and husband over decades. They have mastered the art of presenting their numerical strength as an asset for the support of often cynical and corrupt politicians, without conceding to the constant pressure to become passive vote-banks for specific politicians or political parties. They have earned the envy (and the respect) of commercial builders and land-developers for whom all housing markets in Mumbai are a zone for unhindered profit making; and the grudging regard of politicians and quasi-criminal interests who tend to dominate the real estate and development world of Mumbai. Above all, they have had steady and growing success in eroding the view that the street- and slum-dwelling poor are non-citizens and parasites on the economy of Mumbai, and in forcing politicians, bureaucrats, planners and various urban elites to recognise that the poor cannot be treated as a cancer on the body of the city and are citizens who deserve the same rights as all others and that they are in numerous ways vital to the service and production economies of Mumbai. In short, the various communities and leaders who are at the core of the Alliance have created an irreversible dynamic of 'recognition' (in Charles Taylor's sense) which today makes it impossible to ignore their massive numerical presence and their legitimate rights to housing, to infrastructure and to a political voice in the life of the city.

The cosmopolitan practices of the Alliance have much to do with these hard-won successes. And it can be seen in the most humble as well as the most dramatic of forms. It can be seen in the housing and toilet exhibitions that I discussed in earlier essays on this movement. In these events, which combine festivity, learning, dialogue and solidarity building, women (and men) from different cities and regions encounter each other and make the effort to encompass some of India's linguistic and cultural diversities. They discuss their hopes about domestic space, their experiences with different building materials and techniques, their practices of savings and credit, and more generally their hopes for permanent housing and political security in their streets and cities. Friendships are formed, tragedies are shared, stories are exchanged and experiences of urban struggle are framed to be understood by women for other women who come from different spatial worlds of poverty. Often these exchanges involve linguistic negotiation, as when women from Nepal or Orissa talk to women from Pune or Tamil Nadu, often through the bridging efforts of the polyglot women of Mahila Milan from Mumbai. A single extended collective conversation could involve the use of several varieties of Hindi and Marathi, or Kannada and Oriya and Tamil, and even some English (if visitors from overseas networks of donors are present). Translation is a continuous background activity, as participants gloss and explain exchanges to each other and older and less literate members are told about new social and technical issues. Language in these settings is medium and message, background and foreground, tool and horizon. It is rarely articulated as a site of conscious negotiation or effort. Yet it is the first and most critical site of the effort to stretch the cultural horizons of these poor women and men. It cannot be underestimated as the basis for all other forms of translation, learning and exchange in the work of the global network.

These inter-city occasions within the Indian framework cannot be seen as the main context in which the membership of the Alliance learns the strategies of cosmopolitanism. In fact, the daily struggles to self-organise in Mumbai over the decades from the early 1980s to the present cannot be seen outside the context of the steady will of the poorest members of the Alliance to negotiate and transcend a variety of critical cultural boundaries and thus to create an expanded sense of their own cultural selves. For example, the poorest women who constitute the senior core of Mahila Milan are largely Muslim women from the Telugu-speaking region of Andhra Pradesh, who entered the sex-trade as sex-workers in Nagpada and the adjoining areas of Central Mumbai. Their already complex linguistic and cultural worlds (quite different from the world of the quasi-courtesans of the Muslim North) encountered in Mumbai the brutal world of multilingual male sex-shoppers, corrupt Marathi-speaking policemen, and toilers and brokers speaking every variety of Hindi, Tamil and Gujarati.

As they organised themselves into the self-help group called Mahila Milan to escape their previous professions, learn other modes of livelihood and achieve housing security, they remained for decades confined to pavement dwellings in their original working neighbourhoods. But they also learned to work and cooperate with the largely male membership of the National Slum Dwellers Federation, many of whom are Tamil-speakers from Dharavi and its nearby Tamil-dominated neighbourhoods far to the north of Nagpada. These Tamil-speaking men represented a different set of histories and trajectories, often less than sympathetic to the sex-workers (as most Mumbai males would be) and were also further advanced in the strategies of Mumbai housing politics and civic survival. Emerging from the complex occupational and political world of Dharavi and its environs, they were already fairly skilled in dealing with their own Tamil underworld, with its Muslim extensions (since some of the most prominent members of Mumbai's underworld in the period from 1950 to 1980 were Tamils, both Hindu and Muslim). They were likewise deeply experienced in operating in the fringe world constituted in the nexus of ward politics, crime, police and slum landlords and thus brought a more sophisticated set of political assets to the Alliance. The transactions between these two microcultures in Mumbai (the Muslim female former sex-workers of Mahila Milan and the largely male Tamil-speaking working-class men of the NSDF) already required more than a modest negotiation of cultural styles and gaps in the mosaic of Mumbai's class, language and sexual politics. This ongoing negotiation, which has direct implications for the overall strategies of the Alliance in Mumbai, is one example of the daily struggles to negotiate cultural differences among the poorest of the urban poor in Mumbai. Such cosmopolitanism is hard won, unsupported as it is by the apparatus of literacy, cultural privilege or by the practices of leisure and self-cultivation. In the case of these poor women and men from the slums of Mumbai, what we learn is that dialogue is always a risky business, that nearby Others can be as challenging as distant Others, and that progressive politics can emerge out of the compulsory cosmopolitanism of the wretched of the earth.

Dialogue, Risk and Conviviality

The debates about Gandhian non-violence and the negotiations among the urban poor of Mumbai show us that negotiations across major religions and civilisations like Christianity and Islam have something to learn from 'internal' debates, such as those among Hindus in India about non-violence or about social change among the urban poor in India.

The point of these examples is to make the case that we cannot avoid the risks of dialogue, because dialogue always threatens to hide internal debates or to exaggerate them. To productively manage the risks of dialogue requires us to identify those internal debates which have the greatest consequence for our external debates. In the era of globalisation, it is likely that the subjects which connect internal and external debates are likely to have a lot to do with democracy, free markets, migration, poverty, environment, just war and social welfare. Each of these subjects carries with it very high stakes.

I propose that intercultural or intercivilisational dialogue not be structured so as to avoid these subjects. In that case, intercultural dialogue would become a poor second cousin to diplomacy, warfare and terrorism. True dialogue must take up these major subjects. But it must do so in a prudent way, without denying internal debates or inflating them beyond proportion. Above all, we must pick the right internal debates to bring to the table our external dialogues. The right internal debates can be a sensitive guide to the landscape in which common ground can be found. The wrong ones can take us into the territory of non-negotiable convictions and the clash of totalised ideologies.

In conclusion, all dialogue is risky, because it brings internal and external debates into a common framework. But we have no choice but to accept this risk and to find ways of managing it. In doing so, I suggest a strategy of selectivity, so that we do not force ourselves to share all of our humanity with each other all of the time. The negotiation of the right parts of our humanity with each other is both prudent and sufficient to build a contingent and evolving framework for conviviality. This is true for rich and poor,

Hindus and Muslims, Christians and Jews. Whether they debate within or across their group boundaries, they would be well-advised not to demand the full disclosure of their humanity to one another. Rather, they would be better advised to undertake the risk of dialogue one issue at a time.

Acknowledgements

I am grateful to the Gulbenkian Foundation in Lisbon (Portugal) for their invitation to me to co-curate the symposium on Distance, Proximity and the Other and to deliver the keynote lecture on this occasion. I am especially grateful to President Emílio Rui Vilar, Professor António Pinto Ribeiro and Miguel Magalhaes, as well as the other speakers and members of the audience at the Symposium. I am especially grateful for the remarks and contributions of President Jorge Sampaio, of the Republic of Portugal, who was an acute listener and speaker at this event.

Identity and Violence:
Towards a Critique of Amartya Sen[*]

DIPESH CHAKRABARTY

In 1944, when he was a boy of eleven, Amartya Sen witnessed first-hand some of the Hindu–Muslim violence that tore British India apart on the eve of the partition of the country into India and Pakistan. Kader Mia, a young Muslim day labourer, was knifed by Hindus as he came into Sen's neighbourhood in Dhaka looking for work. The murder has always haunted Sen as an example of a tragic feature that is unfortunately all too common in human societies: killing people for no other reason than the fact that they belong, often by birth, to particular communities. 'For an eleven-year-old child...' writes Sen, 'that Kader Mia should be seen as having only one identity ... seemed altogether incredible.' Why should 'many-sided persons' be seen as 'having exactly one identity each, linked with religion, or more exactly, religious ethnicity'? This murderously fallacious thinking is what Sen confronts in *Identity and Violence* (2006), bringing to bear on his earlier sense of bewilderment the extraordinary powers of his incisive intellect and humanist disposition.

[*] This short essay is based on Amartya Sen's *Identity and Violence: The Illusion of Destiny* (New York: Norton, 2006).

What motivates Sen to revisit a problem he first encountered as a child is the contemporary world in which academics such as Samuel Huntington – the author of the notorious 'clash of civilisations' thesis – and terrorist groups such as Islamic Jihadists or the masters of ethnic violence in Rwanda or Sudan, seem likewise bent on reducing our usually plural sense of identities to one aspect only, whether civilisation or religion. Sen, of course, does not claim that academics and activists advocating 'imaginary singularities' have the same intention. His point is that 'conceptual disarray, and not just nasty intentions, significantly contributes to the turmoil and barbarity we see around us'. To mitigate this, what has to be combated is the 'illusion' of a single culture or religion constituting any kind of 'destiny' for us: 'We have to see clearly that we have many different affiliations ... There is room for us to decide on our priorities.'

Sen's *Identity and Violence* is a collection of essays – ranging far and wide in history – that argues for the importance of conceptual clarity in developing the requisite combat strategies. A rational awareness of our multiple identities in combination with policies promoting such awareness, Sen argues, can help mitigate ethnic hatred. The first half of the book disposes of ideas that see cultures as single, discrete and self-contained, by giving historical examples and arguments to the contrary. Sen has some wonderful vignettes of histories of cross-cultural borrowings – between the Christian West and the Islamic Near East, say – and has much to say on how western colonial rule may have created both the colonising and the colonised mindsets and contributed, respectively, to unhelpful obsessions with themes of western supremacy or western domination. The second part of the book develops Sen's ideas about multiculturalism, cultural diversity versus cultural freedom, tradition and reason, and so on.

If you were a Samuel Huntington or an academic or thinker of similar ilk, and believed that the world's contemporary problems stem from either a 'clash of civilisations' or from some fundamental and long-standing problems that Muslims have had in adjusting to modernity, then you would probably see Sen's book as attempting to drive a formidable and final nail into the coffin of your thesis. Any attempt on your part to resurrect the idea will see you having to struggle hard against the force and absolute reasonableness of most of Sen's claims. With a wealth of examples he demonstrates that what he calls 'the solitarist illusion of identity' – the notion that someone's identity could all be wrapped up in any one domain of life, such as religion – is just that, an illusion. Nobody in the real world, either now or in the past, has ever lived cooped up in only one part of himself. Huntington and others who think like him are prisoners of this 'solitarist' fallacy.

It's also the case, however, that no democratic government has ever officially acted on explicitly Huntingtonian assumptions. If anything, George W. Bush, Tony Blair and John Howard have all gone out of their way to explain that the current war against terror was not a war against Muslims or Islam as such, for either they recognise the plurality of interpretations of Islam or they accept that the preaching of terror is somehow not 'true' Islam. Challenging Huntington is good academic sport; it also makes for conceptual clarity in thinking about the relationship between identity and violence. But what practical purpose does it serve when no elected government acts under its spell?

Sen recognises the question and, as if to answer it, puts forward the second element in his argument, one that has implications for public policy in multicultural states. (His examples, for biographical reasons, are mostly British. I will, for a similar reason, include Australian examples in addition to Indian ones.) He clearly opposes funding for faith-based schools, including schools for 'Muslim, Hindu, and Sikh children', for such a policy 'encourages a fragmentary perception of the demands of living in a desegregated Britain'. 'Education,' he writes, 'is not just about getting children, even very young ones ... inherited ethos. It is also about helping children develop the ability to reason about new decisions any grown-up person will have to make.' Sen also opposes, on similar grounds, the tendency for elected heads of democratic states to treat religious leaders as spokesmen for their communities. He does not dispute Blair's 'dedication to fairness and justice' but disagrees with his decision to 'go out' and 'have debates about terror and peace "inside the Muslim community"'. Here Sen's argument has obvious relevance to democracies generally and should be heard with interest. 'Attempts to tackle terrorism through the aid of religion,' he says with reference to Britain and America, have 'had the effect of magnifying ... the voice of Islamic clerics ... on matters that are not in the domain of religion, at a time when the political and social roles of Muslims in civil society, including in the practice of democracy, need emphasis and much greater support.'

Sen's points about the need to bolster civil society and state institutions − and ensuring that the rule of law holds − are generally pertinent to the contemporary world. But some questions remain. What if, say, in a multicultural society such as Australia, Muslims spontaneously and substantially organise themselves through their mosques (I know that Australian Hindus have often in the past formed themselves into Temple Societies or other similar organisations), while their representation in civil society organisations is weak? Can governments afford to wait until their activity in civil society institutions becomes strong, and not speak to 'communities' till then? Sen grants the pragmatic part of the problem. His example is Iraq but the argument I think applies to Australia as well. He thinks, for instance, that it has been a mistake on the part of the US-led Coalition to view Iraq 'as a sum total of communities' (Shia, Sunni, Kurd) and work for the representation of each in the national government. 'This was certainly the *easiest* [my emphasis] way to proceed, given the tensions that already existed in the country and ... the new ones the occupation itself had created.' But his argument is a principled rather than a pragmatic one: 'the easiest way in the short run,' he contends, 'is not the best way to build the future of a country' if the aspiration is to a 'conglomeration of citizens, rather than a collectivity of religious ethnicities'.

It is in this interesting prescription that I see both the strengths and the weaknesses of Sen's position. His argument rests on an implicit dichotomy of pragmatism and principle that is too strong to register the messiness of actual histories (and futures) − the fact that they may present a messy compromise somewhere between those two poles. One could argue, for instance, that mosques, particularly under the pressure of current politics in countries like

Australia, are themselves taking on some of the characteristics of organisations in civil society. Witness the electoral process that now attends the selection of a mufti in Sydney – clearly, the very formation of the Muslim community in Sydney is being profoundly influenced by some kind of cultural dialogue with other sections of Australian society. This would not have happened without the 'pragmatic' liaison between government and community organisations that was prompted by the exigencies of the post-9/11 situation. In other words, changes that were initiated on pragmatic grounds may result in making for some permanent and principled changes as well. Sen, however, does not even consider this middle position.

My main problem with Sen's framework has to do with its relationship – or its non-relationship, if I may put it that way – with actual histories. In the binaries through which he wants to view the world – conservatism versus choice, tradition versus reason – actual history is often the missing third position. His historical examples are, really, a collection of instances from various parts of the world chosen to bolster his abstract points. He pays very little attention to the nature of historical processes. Not that he is required to, but the omission has implications for his argument.

'There are,' says Sen on the issue of multiculturalism, 'two basically distinct approaches ... one of which concentrates on the promotion of diversity as a value in itself; the other approach focuses on reasoning and decision-making, and celebrates cultural diversity to the extent that it is as freely chosen as possible by the persons involved.' A few pages on, he gives an example. 'If a young girl in a conservative immigrant family wants to go out on a date with an English boy, that would certainly be a multicultural initiative. In contrast, the attempt by her guardians to stop her from doing this ... is hardly a multicultural move, since it seeks to keep the cultures sequestered.' Or, as he observes earlier: 'young women from conservative immigrant families in the West might be kept on a short leash by the elders for fear that they would emulate the freer lifestyle of the majority community. Diversity would then be achieved at the cost of cultural liberty.'

Such incidents, one may agree with Sen, are common enough

to constitute a good class of examples, not only in Britain but also in Australia. But in reality parental attempts to stop daughters from forming relationships outside the community could take a range of forms, from confining the girl physically to reasoning with her. In the extreme case of physical violence or restriction — the 'short leash' of Sen's description, literally speaking — his argument would clearly hold. But many cases will not be so extreme. And the forms of reasoning between parents and children might include both rational and non-rational means of persuasion on both sides. Now if, as a result of such reasoning and discussion, the daughter decided not to go ahead with this particular relationship, could we automatically and immediately conclude whether this was or was *not* a case of cultural freedom?

Sen allows for the fact that one's choices may be influenced by one's 'social origin and background', but one must make one's 'own decisions and choose [one's] own priorities'. But how does one ever know if one has reached a point where there is a clear separation between the influences of one's social origins and the sphere of one's 'own decisions'? Most people have to live with a degree of indeterminacy on this question. We can, in defining freedom, agree on abstract values. Suppose we value the idea of individual autonomy. In deciding what kind of behaviour will constitute individual autonomy in particular contexts, we have recourse to a repertoire of behaviour that is for the most part culturally given, so that even in exercising our own reason and choice, we choose between available cultural alternatives. The choice between 'inheritance' and 'reason' in many cases will not be an absolute one. Historical processes will situate us in the middle somewhere, while Sen's arguments seem tailored more for extreme situations.

I find a similar foreshortening of historical processes occurring in Sen's analysis of the relation between identity and violence in situations of ethnic or religious carnage. To make my point, let me stay with cases of violence that I know best: Hindu–Muslim riots in the distant and recent Indian past. Sen clearly thinks that the butchery of pogroms, carnage and riots are enabled by the solitarist fallacy of identity. People suddenly come to see themselves and their Others as possessing, not multiple and contextual, but single and context-free identities. At the beginning of the book, Sen claims that 'violence is fomented by the imposition of singular and belligerent identities on gullible people, championed by proficient artisans of terror'. Speaking of the murder victim Kader Mia, Sen notes that the young boy labourer was

> a Muslim, and no other identity was relevant to the vicious Hindu thugs who had pounced on him ... The political instigators who urged the killing ... managed to persuade many otherwise peaceable people of both communities to turn into dedicated thugs. They were made to think of themselves only as Hindus or only as Muslims ... and absolutely nothing else: not Indians, not subcontinentals, not Asians, not as members of a shared human race.

Does such a process of categorical disarray, inherent, say, in the Huntington thesis, really accompany communal riots in India (and elsewhere)? There is no question that when a Hindu kills a Muslim for being Muslim, or vice versa, the killing happens because of the way a person's affiliation to a group is perceived. Sen is right to draw our attention to the problem of how violence may be related to issues pertaining to one's identity. But the processes involved in determining someone's affiliation during a time of riot and in 'normal' times would appear to be rather different processes, and an argument that works well against a Huntington may not be able to capture the difference at issue. Here, again, it is Sen's ethnography – or the lack of any ethnographic instinct in Sen's analytic framework – that I find unsatisfactory. Let me explain a little further.

Usually, as Sen himself documents, when they are *not* engaged in making scapegoats out of each other for various imagined or real ills that have befallen them, Hindus and Muslims are quite aware of their multiple and contextual identities. Actual examples from riots would suggest that these complex understandings of identities are not necessarily forgotten at times of riots. Rather, there comes into play in the murderous exchanges between members of antagonistic communities a process that is perhaps better described as *identification* than as 'identity'.[1]

'Identity' relates to our own sense of self in everyday life. It is by nature complex and allows for plural affiliations. Human beings, I agree with Sen, cannot live otherwise. It seems to be a perfectly acceptable proposition that all functioning human beings have plural understandings of themselves, derived from the various roles and contexts they inhabit and the exchanges they engage in their usual, everyday life. Identity thus has to do with my own understanding and thus with my interiority. I carry it within myself. 'Identification', however, refers to the external and surface signs by which I or others might identify myself as a member of a particular group: my skull cap, my turban, my beard, my name, my clothes, my circumcised or uncircumcised penis. Thus, while 'identity' refers to processes going on inside myself – they answer to the question of how I see myself – 'identification' is a social process that is, usually, as much a part of my everyday life as are the processes that have to do with my identity.

I may or may not be an observing Muslim, and that may be critical to my own identity, but is not necessarily critical to how I am identified. Anecdotes or ethnographic accounts of the mass psychology of rioting in the subcontinent always show this process of *identification* (of the Muslim or the Hindu) overriding issues of *identity* during the charged, frenzied and lunatic conditions of mass murder, rape, pillage and burning. People are killed not because of their identities but because of the way they are identified.

That this is not hair splitting will be clear if we look, for example, at the butchery of Muslims by Hindu crowds (organised by Hindu extremist organisations and political leaders) in Gujarat in February 2002. About a thousand Muslims were tortured and killed – and tens of thousands rendered homeless – in retaliation for an attack on pilgrims on a train in which about fifty-eight Hindus, many of them women and children, had been burnt to death. The *Hindustan Times* of 4 March 2002 reported the case of a Muslim boy who had been left for dead by Hindu assailants. Brought to a hospital by a passerby who found him 'badly burnt' on the street, the boy refused to give his Muslim name to the hospital authority as he was clearly afraid of the features by which he could be identified as a Muslim. He wanted to be called by a Hindu name, Prasad. *Bataa sale kya hai, Hindu ya mian* – 'Tell us, you bastard, what are you: Hindu or Muslim?' – the thugs had demanded of Prasad's family on Ring Road. The mob wanted to take their pants off to see if they were circumcised. But they did not need to: 'one among the mob had got his hands on an identity card bearing Prasad's brother's [Muslim] name ... *Arrey, mian hai, mian* ['Hey, he is a Muslim!'], he had exulted in murderous triumph', and the butchery followed. (Here's a clear case where '*identification* card' would be a more apt usage.)

Even visitors who came to the hospital to see Prasad would not give their Muslim names. It does not mean that they had forgotten their identities. There is no reason to assume that they had forgotten the complex sense of identity that marked 'normal' everyday life. But they were scared of being *identified* as Muslims in the same way that many Jewish families in Nazi Europe tried to save themselves by repressing things that would mark them out as Jews. Prasad pleaded with his doctors to address him as a Hindu: 'They will kill me if they find out I survived. Don't tell anyone I am a Muslim, I beg of you.'²

Or take the case of Muslim shopkeepers in Ahmedabad and Vadodara who, to escape overnight looting and burning of their shops by Hindu rioters, painted images of Hindu gods on their 'rusted shutters' or hung boards proclaiming: 'This shop belongs to a Hindu.'³ As with so-called identity cards, signs on shops are not markers of identities; they are means of identification. Clearly, what was at issue in this instance was how these shops were going to be *identified* by the rioters, not the actual identities of the owners of the shops.

What I am saying here will not, I suspect, surprise Sen. He will be as aware of these processes as anyone else. Why, then, does he still hope that the armoury of conceptual clarity that he deploys against the confused thinking of a Huntington would also act as an antidote to 'the turmoil and barbarity we see around us' generally? To the extent that Sen has things to say about religion and its place in public life in democracies, about the need to strengthen civil society organisations by making them inclusive and non-racist, he, of course, offers us reasons for hope. His insights into the role that our thoughts about our identities may play in fomenting or encouraging ethnic violence have obvious merit. But it may be helpful, in thinking about large-scale ethnic violence, to distinguish between our own mental processes through which we form images of ourselves as bearing multiple identities, and the social processes by which we get identified as belonging to one or another group. Such marking by the Other can happen both informally and officially, as when governments identify and label people in the interest of distribution of benefits and services.

There is a liberal common sense that recognises or at least documents the existence of the two processes and yet assumes that social proofs of people having 'multiple identities' would somehow stop them from engaging in ethnic violence or cleansing. Let me end by citing a recent report in the Indian newspaper *Times of India* relating to the celebration of a Sufi festival, *Phool Walon ki Sair*, on 23 October 2008 at the dargah of Khawja Syed Qutbuddin Bakhtiyar Khaki in the Mehrauli area of New Delhi. This is a festival that, reportedly, has come down from the Mughal times. The British banned it in 1942 and the Indian Prime Minister Nehru revived it – precisely as a festival marking Hindu–Muslim harmony – in 1961. The report described the participation of Hindu men, women and girls in the festival and quotes a certain Mirza Mohtaram Bakht, the secretary of the Anjuman Sair-e-Gul Faroshan, as saying to the reporter: 'The festival is a clear message to the dividing forces that we are stronger than them. Look around: can you tell the difference between a Hindu and a Muslim?' That question – 'Look around: can you tell the difference between a Hindu and a Muslim?' – is clearly a recognition of, as well as a challenge to, the social processes of labelling that I have called here identification. The questioner's rhetoric accepts that such processes exist and it points to their irrationality, as it were. Somehow, the assumption is that if Hindus and Muslims participate in each other's festivities, it will make it easier for them to recognise their multiple identities and thus desist from killing each other. Looking on such rational thinking as an antidote to violence is not very far away from a belief that ethnic conflict is an outbreak of irrational thinking that can be combated by rational thought. The same newspaper report ends by quoting a young man, Manish, a Hindu, who informally acts as a teacher in the neighbourhood and who, according to the report, 'firmly believe[s] that modern education is one way of combating militancy'. (He obviously does not remember 'techie' jihadists.) He is quoted as saying: 'I teach Science and Maths to the kids here; hopefully, they will grow up to be rational adults, not extremists.'[4]

It is this idea that considers ethnic violence to be the result of irrational thinking that I am addressing here. Everyday life is made up of a mixture of both identity-related processes and processes of identification. When ethnic killing and violence happen, it is the processes of identification that come into play, unmitigated by the processes that go into the making of identities. It is perhaps fallacious to think that there is continuity between 'everyday life' in which identity and identification processes coexist without any competition between them and moments of violence when processes relating to identity formation are overridden by those of identification. This assumption of a continuous social life that extends from one moment to another is what seems to call for further investigation and questioning.

Notes

1 I am indebted to some of Arjun Appadurai's writings in thinking about questions of identification.

2 This case is documented in Nandini Sundar, 'A License to Kill: Patterns of Violence in Gujarat', in Siddharth Varadarajan (ed.), *Gujarat: The Making of a Tragedy* (Delhi: Penguin, 2002), p. 104.

3 *Report of the Human Rights Watch (New York)*, reproduced in M.L. Sondhi and Apratim Mukherjee (eds), *The Black Book of Gujarat* (Delhi: Manak, 2002), Part B, p. 245.

4 'Where Religion does not Define Identity', *Times of India*, 23 October 2008, at http://timesofindia.indiatimes.com/ (accessed 23 October 2008).

Literature and Intercultural Dialogue

EUNICE DE SOUZA

I would like to begin this talk on Literature and Intercultural Dialogue by reading a poem which I think appropriate for the occasion. It is by Nissim Ezekiel, perhaps our best-known Indian poet writing in English. It is called 'Talking', and the epigraph for the poem is by Paul Blackburn who writes,

> Why has life put such
> a need to talk inside us
> when there is no one to talk to?

Ezekiel's poem reads:

> There's all humanity to talk to,
> there's also you.
>
> I'm not afraid of being
> misunderstood. When I talk
> because I must, the landscape
> overflows with figures who want

to listen. United by our ignorance
we struggle, and the words
materialize, begin to matter.
Is this surprising, unusual?
Not at all. Language
is our conspicuous gift: the Word,
made flesh, is sought again.
We make it as we make our lives.

There's also you,
who speak for yourself
and must be listened to.[1]

The poem embodies exactly the themes of this conference, the need for and scope of dialogue, awareness of the Other. And, given the fact that it is written by a poet, it demonstrates the role literature can play in this dialogue, despite the many factors that can militate against an individual voice that does not conform to accepted patterns. I intend to look at some of the factors that militate against dialogue, and against individual artistic voices in India, and also to look at what, if anything, writers can do in such an atmosphere. I am specifically concerned with the prejudice against writers in India who write in English.

For a variety of reasons, some negative, and others which appear to be positive, the political and cultural climate of our country is not exactly geared to dialogue at the moment, and I am not sure when and how this will change. More than fifty years after India gained Independence, who or what is Indian still remains a contested concept. I will illustrate this with a small but not untypical incident. I was reading in the library of the University of Bombay a few years ago when a person at the next table asked me my name. When I told him what it was, he was startled, and said, 'I thought you were Indian.' I don't think he intended to be offensive. He was just using 'Indian' as a synonym for 'Hindu', as many people continue to do. Presumably, he associated Christians with western dresses, hats, gloves and stockings! Or, as sometimes happens in Bollywood films, the loose secretary in a very mini skirt indeed, out to seduce the good Hindu boy. Ironically, this incident took place when I was researching that very concept 'Indianness', and attempting to work out what exactly was meant by it.

In a situation such as ours in contemporary India, an ex-colony with plural traditions, involved in the process of modernising yet seeking to retain what is valuable, it is natural that, both at a socio-cultural level and in the field of the arts and literature, there is concern with what constitutes 'Indianness'. Running through the entire debate are the tensions of the East–West encounter, and the desire to find 'fixed points of reference in the enlarged world of today'. What can we call authentically Indian? Is it parochial and outdated to be concerned with such a concept? Can we arrive at a definition of 'Indianness' which is distinct yet flexible enough not to become a weapon for exclusion? We have so many weapons of exclusion already: religion, caste, gender, language, economic status. After Independence, states were created according to linguistic lines. Now there are demands for more states to be carved out of existing ones on the basis of ethnic groupings.

Numerous scholars have written on the problem of isolating authentic Indian elements. One of them offers a useful summary.

The inheritance that India has stepped into is only partly Hindu and Indian. Its mental background and equipment, though largely influenced by the persistence of Indian traditions, have been moulded into their present shape by over a hundred years of Western education extending practically to every field of mental activity. The social ideas are not what Hindu society had for long cherished but those assimilated from the West and derived predominantly from the doctrines of the French Revolution, and to a lesser extent the teaching of Marx and the lessons of the Soviet experiment... The New Indian State represents traditions, ideals, and principles which are the results of an effective but imperfect synthesis between the East and the West.[2]

Actually, there is no consensus among scholars about what constitutes essential features of Indianness. Some scholars have included among the essential features of Indian culture the qualities of tolerance, a capacity for synthesis, a universal outlook, a philosophical outlook, respect for the individual, a strong social sense and an open attitude to science. Others, however, say exactly the opposite, and see Hinduism as essentially authoritarian, discounting individuality and free enquiry. The much-vaunted tolerance is seen as indifference rather than as respect for the other person's right to be different. These essentialist attempts continue, despite what is obvious – that, as the historian Romila Thapar has pointed out, what may appear to be the essentials of a culture may in fact be what concerned ideologues wish to portray as essentials. Indian history has been interpreted by Orientalists, utilitarians, nationalists and communalists posing as nationalists.[3] To each his own distortion! The unqualified praise of India by Orientalists such as Max Mueller who never visited India has done as much damage as the negative accounts of some utilitarians. Some postcolonial critics too have distorted history to justify their anti-British senti-ments. They claim, for instance, that English was forced down Indian throats in colonial times, though the evidence points to the opposite. Generally, anything approved of is regarded as Indian, while anything disapproved of is regarded as western.

Women and women writers were, and continue to be, in many ways victims of the concern with Indianness even though many women joined the nationalist struggle. A Hindi writer, Mridula Garg, has written, 'We might have been put to a harder test then but the issue at stake was much simpler. Getting rid of foreign rule. Not domination. Domination can continue in subtle, complex and devious forms, after the rule is over. And it is much more difficult to fight.'[4] Political activists fighting for independence were not necessarily in favour of social reform for women, or even their participation in politics. Geraldine Forbes tells us that the husband of a woman who was arrested sent word to the jail that she was not to return home after being released.[5] It was an honour to have a wife arrested, he told the person who tried to intervene, but she had not sought permission to leave the house. Partha Chatterjee says that the strategy employed was to stress the spiritual superi-ority of Indians by putting the onus on women to preserve 'tradition'. Women had to talk, dress, eat and generally behave in a way that clearly distinguished them from western women, certainly, but especially from the alleged obnoxiousness of westernized Indian women.[6] Kamaladevi Chattopadhyay, a radical in many ways, felt that women could never be free under colonialism, because the history of British imperialism was 'one unbroken chain of betrayals'.[7] But her view is belied in Independent India as even a cursory look at the news will show. And 'tradition', defined in essentialist and narrow terms has, unsurprisingly, turned demagogic, reactionary and violent.

Today, a politically inspired agitation against Valentine's Day may seem foolish, but the violence that accompanies it is often vicious. At the same time, foreign brands in clothes and technology flourish here. More seriously, Mumbai, once a liberal and cosmopolitan city, is in danger of becoming completely parochial, again because of political parties that don't want 'outsiders' in the city. 'Outsiders' once meant South Indians; in the last year or so it has meant North Indians, many of whom were terrorised into leaving the city. If institutions or individual scholars express views contrary to current political beliefs, the institutions are vandalised, scholars threatened or physically attacked, and books are banned. There is an atmosphere of increasing fear and self-censorship that has begun to take over the city and parts of the country. Fundamentalists of all religious persuasions now appear to set the agenda. As elsewhere, and by now this is old news, the big divide is not really between East and West so much as between fundamentalists and liberals in both camps. An Indian scholar who teaches in Canada makes this point: 'I believe,' Arun P. Mukherjee says in an essay called 'Some Uneasy Conjectures', 'that even though post-colonial theory positions itself as the discourse of liberation, it is of no use to those whose battle is with homegrown oppressors. In fact, it works against them because, in the post-colonial parlance, these homegrown oppressors become "the oppressed" who get all the post-colonialist's sympathy for their suffering at the hand of the colonizer.'[8] She comments further on the uncomfortable resemblance between the rhetoric of postcolonialism and that of cultural fundamentalism. 'If I were to use the language of post-colonialist theory,' she says, 'I would describe the efforts of the BJP/VHP intelligentsia as "resisting" the discourse of the so-called Muslim colonizers of India.'[9]

Of course, such threats do not come merely from fundamentalists. The cry of 'Indian' may be raised in a war, or critical remarks made by another country, or even when the Indian side is playing cricket or taking part in the Olympics or international beauty contests, or when an Indian wins the Nobel Prize, or the Magsaysay Award, makes a scientific discovery, or becomes an astronaut. The media are full of stories about Indian millionaires abroad, and about the economic resurgence of this country. 'Shining India' is now a popular slogan. Such euphoria may seem natural, but there is something a little suspect, for instance, when we are so eager to claim as Indian people who migrated years ago and achieved what they could elsewhere. What is more, the euphoria doesn't translate us into a more mature society. If a cricketer does badly in a crucial game, his house is burnt down. Rabindranath Tagore may have won the Nobel Prize, but his statements on violence go unheeded. He tells us about the storm generated by an article he once wrote about his belief that 'we must win our country, not from some foreigner, but from our own inertia, our own indifference'.[10] He says it was not merely journalists who attacked him but 'even men of credit and courtesy were unable to speak of me in restrained language'.[11] He talks of the many policies with which he did not agree: the burning of foreign cloth, the encouragement given to schoolchildren to leave their books and join in the movement, the boycott of Manchester, the partition of Bengal. In those days, he says, 'there was practically nothing to stand in the way of the spirit of destructive revel, which spread all over the country. We went about picketing, burning, placing thorns in the path of those whose way was not ours, acknowledging no restraints in language or behaviour.'[12] It was his misfortune, Tagore says, that when everyone was full of righteous anger he appeared on the scene 'with my doubts and my attempts to divert the current... My only success was in diverting their wrath on to my own devoted head.'[13]

Where does literature (itself a contested concept) and its allied concerns such as literary criticism come into all this? After all, literature ideally is a space where individual voices reflect personal and social experience and perspectives, without having to conform to prescribed frameworks. I have just quoted Tagore saying that he attempted to divert the current with his doubts. Though he was talking about a journalistic article he wrote, what he says applies to all writers. They question received truths, explore the complexities of an experience, personal and social, express what others may not be able to express.

Or they show us, as Aravind Adiga has, the brutal face of our essentially feudal country, in which poverty and corruption are rife, and a man's entire extended family can be slaughtered for a wrong which he is perceived to have done. There is a long, moving passage in which the narrator recalls his mother's funeral, and it encapsulates the sadness of the book, and its sense of the darkness in which we live, that no one may question received truths and the caste-ridden destinies in which we are born. 'My mother's body had been wrapped from head to toe in a saffron silk cloth, which was covered in rose petals and jasmine garlands,' the narrator says.

> I don't think she ever had such a fine thing to wear in her life... As the fire ate away the satin, a pale foot jerked out, like a living thing; the toes, which were melting in the heat, began to curl up, offering resistance to what was being done to them. Kusum shoved the foot into the fire, but it would not burn. My heart began to race. My mother wasn't going to let them destroy her. Underneath the platform with the piled-up fire logs, there was a giant oozing mound of black mud where the river washed the shore... I looked at the ooze, and I looked at my mother's flexed foot, and I understood.[14]

My concern in this paper is with the way cultural fundamentalism, in the guise of something called 'nativism', has contaminated the literary milieu in India, and led, not to cultural dialogue but cultural confrontation. Specifically, I am concerned with the situation of Indian poets who write in English, and the hostility and contempt with which many Indian writers in the vernaculars view them.

In the nationalist struggle, from the mid-nineteenth century to 1947 when India gained Independence, hostility to English as a medium was perhaps understandable, though even then there were divisions between political leaders. Mahatma Gandhi saw the study of English as a form of enslavement. He opted for Hindi as the national language, and by that word meant Hindustani, the language of both Hindus and Muslims used in Northern India. But Nehru knew that the South would never accept this as a national language. In contrast to Gandhi, he saw English as a 'vitaliser'[15] to our lives, languages and literature. It was western missionaries in different parts of India who aided the development of the vernaculars by bringing in printing presses and publishing dictionaries and various kinds of books, including the Bible, in the vernaculars. Writers in the regional languages adopted many of the forms learned through English literature: the realist novel, prose, blank verse, the sonnet. (And indeed, the very notions of democracy and freedom came to us through western texts.) Contemporary writers in the regional languages acknowledge a wide range of western writers as influences. What is more, it was the first writer of Indian poetry in English, Henry Derozio (1809–31), who was of partly Portuguese origin, who first formulated, in poetry written in English, the idea of a nation. Dr Rosinka Chaudhuri, who has written on Derozio, said to me in an interview about him,

> When Derozio, in 1827, wrote his sonnets to India, which he called 'my native land', he was setting in motion a process that resulted ultimately in shaping the manner in which we think of India… For me, Derozio is an important figure not only because he was the first poet to self-consciously identify himself as an Indian, but because he is a living example in the history of heterogeneity of race, language, creed that may comprise a true-born Indian.[16]

A further paradox is that poets in English in the nineteenth century explored many social themes long before writers in other languages in India. However, towards the last quarter of the nineteenth century some writers who had begun by writing in English changed to the vernacular and urged others to do the same.

But these attitudes have now hardened into what is called 'nativism'. According to the nativists, writing in English is invalid by definition. No foreign language can capture the soul of India. Certainly, in their view, writers who are urban, westernized, and therefore out of touch with India's heritage cannot write authentically about India. Vilas Sarang, who writes in Marathi and in English, says that when reading Indian poetry in English, 'the feeling remains in the reader's mind that superstitions about crows or that detail about the cow, was selected, at least partly, for its exotic appeal to the non-Indian reader. Poets in the Indian languages are free of this bedevilment, for they do not have to flaunt their Indianness before their very Indian readers.'[17] U.R. Ananthamurthy, a novelist who writes in Kannada, says, 'All Indian writers who write in the regional languages have access to the deep springs of life. Because our language is truly preserved there. Television and media cannot affect the Indian language writer as much as it does English writers...'[18] The question of dialogue doesn't arise as they barely read the work of writers in English. Ka Naa Subramanyam, a poet who writes in Tamil, once wrote a poem called 'Situation', which he himself translated into English, showering contempt on 'westernized' Indians generally, and depicting them as mimic men. It reads:

Introduced
to the Upanishads
by T S Eliot;

and to Tagore
by the early
Pound;

and to the Indian Tradition
by Max Mueller
(late of the Bhavan);

and to

Indian dance
by Bowers;

and to
Indian art
by what's his-name;

and to the Tamil classics
by Danielou
(or was it Pope?):

neither flesh
nor fish blood
nor totem-pole;

vociferous
in thoughts
not his own;

eloquent in words
not his own
('The age demanded...')[19]

The concept has occurred in the writings of Indian academics,
again in relation to writing in English in India. The writer in
English emerges from these assessments as a figure either patron-
ised or mistakenly praised by the West, and disliked by writers and
critics in India. He is alienated in the negative sense of the term,
snobbish, empty, his motives for writing suspect, his work irrelevant and written for an irrelevant audience. It is claimed that such
success as he meets with comes in the way of the recognition due
to writers in the Indian languages.

This cultural fundamentalism in the work of academic critics is
evident in statements such as, 'The Indian poet in English can be
a poet only by being truly an Indian.'[20] What this academic has in
mind becomes clearer in another of his books when he contrasts
'Poets rooted (however rebelliously) in the Hindu tradition' with

a 'strong school of ethnic minorities [who] have found the situation in modern India a fertile ground for alienation'.[21] According to him, 'the acid test ... is "could only an Indian have written this?"'[22] The poet R. Parthasarathy talks of the best-known of post-Independence poets, Nissim Ezekiel, in similar terms. He claims that Ezekiel's background, which is Jewish, 'severely circumscribes his poetry ... and this makes him an isolated figure among Indian poets in English, many of whom are Hindus, and who, therefore, can identify themselves with India's past'.[23] In contrast, he says, a poet such as A.K. Ramanujan who knows Kannada and other Indian languages, but writes in English offers the 'first indisputable evidence of the *validity* of Indian English verse'.[24]

At the time I spoke to some poets writing in English to find out what they had to say on these matters. Gieve Patel, who is a doctor, a painter, a playwright and poet, said, 'All this categorizing and putting into columns is the job of scholars, since they have to find some framework. Those frameworks are really fantasies. Writers don't function like that. I admire Ramanujan's work but I don't think it is good because he has access to Hindu culture. That doesn't make him better. He happens to be a very good poet who is using that material.'[25]

The poet Adil Jussawalla says,

I don't know why someone who feels more rooted than me should feel strongly against that. It's a valid experience and many have written on it. The literature of displacement is quite central to 20th century literature. One can't imagine 20th century literature without it. The first time I came back from England I took almost a Hindu nationalist position. I read as many books on Hinduism as I could, became quite anti-West. But it didn't result in writing I liked. It was propagandist. My first book is about life as I saw it abroad. It seems to me important to respond to one's immediate surroundings rather than to take cultural attitudes.[26]

For Nissim Ezekiel, the charge of alienation is, he says,

simple-minded, inverted snobbery: the 'natives' playing the same game as those who thought familiarity with English manners, history etc. was everything. I don't relish either extreme. What is worth discussing is in between, where one could have some kind of struggle with one's environment, language, cultural limitations in order to arrive at a productive and valuable relationship with them. If alienation means desolate, lost etc. one can't imagine living that kind of life. But suppose I object to the fact that virtually everyone in India spits in public, how does being critical of this mean the same as being alienated? I cannot accept the charge of alienation as a way of dismissing a critical voice.[27]

Poets writing in English have increasingly ignored the constant jibes against them, as is evident in this poem by Gieve Patel called 'The Ambiguous Fate of Gieve Patel, He Being neither Muslim nor Hindu in India'. The poem reads:

> To be no part of this hate is deprivation.
> Never could I claim a circumcised butcher
> Mangled a child out of my arms, never rave
> At the milk-bibing grass-guzzling hypocrite
> Who pulled off my mother's voluminous
> Robes and sliced away at her dugs.
> Planets focus their fires
> Into a worm of destruction
> Edging along the continent. Bodies
> Turn ashen and shrivel. I
> Only burn my tail.[28]

Perhaps the strangest example of this prejudice occurs in relation to the work of Arun Kolatkar who writes in both Marathi and English. According to the critical tenets I have mentioned, Arun Kolatkar should be considered an 'insider', as he is a Hindu. But his first book of poems *Jejuri*, which in one sense is about a place of pilgrimage, was attacked for its 'sardonic humour in sizing up the gods in Jejuri'.[29] For this critic, Kolatkar's 'sensibilities have been formed by Western civilization'.[30] Apparently Kolatkar 'does not have distinguishing qualities to enable us to see in him a Maharashtrian if not an Indian'.[31]

It is astonishing how often those who claim to be the true heirs of Indian culture forget cultural history in their hurry to condemn writers in English. With reference to Kolatkar's alleged irreverence at a place of pilgrimage, for instance, they forget that the entire medieval bhakti tradition, of personal devotion to a god, was created by 'outsiders', that is, people who were not Brahmins, were often of the lowest castes, who did not know Sanskrit, were not allowed to read the Vedas, and in some cases even enter temples. As Kolatkar pointed out, in Tukaram, one of the greatest saint-poets,

> In bhakti poetry there is a total debunking of attitudes to worship. One can find this even in Kabir. Tukaram says in a place of pilgrimage you will find stones and water. Only good people contain God. Kabir says that if one were to reach God by worshipping a stone he would rather worship a mountain any day. Or isn't it better to worship a grinding stone instead since it feeds the whole world? They were trying to re-define a genuine religious stance.[32]

These are only a few instances in which it would appear history, including literary history, has been forgotten by those who claim to be true heirs of 'Indian' culture.

So what is an Indian poem? That is the title of a short, sharp essay written by the poet Arvind Krishna Mehrotra. In it he talks about two versions of the same poem (or sequence of poems) written by Arun Kolatkar. In the first version he uses a Mumbai patois which mixes English words with local vernaculars. In English, the version was called 'Three Cups of Tea' and uses American English. I quote from the first part of the poem:

> I want my pay I said
> to the manager
> you'll get paid said

the manager
but not before the first
don't you know the rules?
coolly I picked up his
wrist watch
that lay on the table
wanna bring in the cops
I said
'cordin to my rules
listen baby
I get paid when I say so.[33]

Talking of Kolatkar, Arvind Krishna Mehrotra says that he had a mind which 'could move with ease from first-century BC Italy to eighth-century China to fifteenth-century France to twentieth-century America, while at the same time picking up the language spoken in the backstreets of Bombay'.[34] He kept lists of the authors he read each year, and against 1965 he mentions many poets that writers in India were reading at the time: Berryman, Snyder, Williams, Apollinaire, Catullus and so on. The one exception, Mehrotra says, is the name Belli. In the mid-1960s there was only one translation of this poet around, and it's the one Kolatkar must have read. William Carlos Williams wrote the preface and commented on the translations by Harold Norse. 'These translations are not made into English but into the American idiom in which they appear in the same relationship facing English as the original Roman dialect does to classic Italian.'[35] Mehrotra is pretty certain that Kolatkar made the translation from the poem in Mumbai patois to demotic American English after reading the Belli translation. 'So there it is, your Indian poem,' Mehrotra writes. 'It was written in a Bombay patois by a poet who otherwise wrote in Marathi and English. It then became part of two literatures, Marathi and Indian English, but entered the latter in a translation made in the American idiom, one of whose sources, or, if you will, inspirations, was an American translation of a nineteenth-century Roman poet.'[36]

How do we get out of the morass I have described? As always,

I think it is only through individual contact, even if this individual contact between writers in the vernaculars and those in English is sporadic. For instance, the Income Tax department organises a literary seminar every year because so many writers work in this department. A few poets are always invited from outside the department. On one occasion, I made friends with a fiction writer who writes in Oriya, and we now exchange books, views, mail and so on. There are some opportunities for this at mixed language readings and translation workshops. For the rest, I must end with a poem in English by G.J.V. Prasad who sees no way out of the morass. In a poem called 'Desperately Seeking India' he writes about the way Indians from one part of India are regarded in another:

In Delhi
Without a visa
In Madras
An Aryan spy

Kashmir's no vacation
They tell me it's a nation
And Punjab wants to die

In Bombay
I'm an invader
In Assam
An exploiting trader

They would throw me
From the hills
Kick me
From the plains

I promise
Never
to mention India again.[37]

Notes

1 Nissim Ezekiel, 'Talking', in *Collected Poems 1952−1988* (New Delhi: Oxford University Press, 1989), p. 171.

2 K.N. Pannikar, *The Foundations of New India* (London: George Allen & Unwin, 1963), pp. 15−16.

3 Romila Thapar, Harbans Mukhia and Bipin Chandra, *Communalism and the Writing of Indian History* (New Delhi: People's Publishing House, 1984), p. 61.

4 Mridula Garg, 'My World, My Writing', in Jasbir Jain (ed.), *Growing Up as a Woman Writer* (New Delhi: Sahitya Akademi, 2007), p. 47.

5 Geraldine Forbes, *The New Cambridge History of India IV.2 Women in Modern India* (Cambridge: Cambridge University Press, 2000), p. 121.

6 Partha Chatterjee, *The Nation and Its Fragments* (New Delhi: Oxford University Press, 1997), pp. 126−7.

7 Kamaladevi Chattopadhyay, 'Education and Child Marriage', in *The Awakening of Indian Women* (Madras: Everyman's Press, 1939), p. 13.

8 Arun P. Mukherjee, 'Some Uneasy Conjectures', in Harish Trivedi and Meenakshi Mukherjee (eds), *Interrogating Post-Colonialism* (Shimla: Indian Institute of Advanced Studies, 1996), p. 17.

9 Mukherjee, 'Some Uneasy Conjectures', p. 19.

10 R.K. Prabhu and Ravindra Kelekar (eds), *Truth Called Them Differently: Tagore−Gandhi Controversy* (Ahmedabad: Navajivan Publishing House, 1961), p. 47.

11 Prabhu and Kelekar (eds), *Truth Called Them Differently*, p. 48.

12 Prabhu and Kelekar (eds), *Truth Called Them Differently*, p. 48.

13 Prabhu and Kelekar (eds), *Truth Called Them Differently*, p. 49.

14 Aravind Adiga, *The White Tiger* (Noida: HarperCollins, 2008), pp. 16−17.

15 Introduction to Arvind Krishna Mehrotra (ed.), *An Illustrated History of Indian Literature in English* (New Delhi: Permanent Black, 2003), p. 15.

16 Dr Rosinka Chaudhuri, interview with the author, *Mumbai Mirror*, 29 December 2007, p. 31.

17 Vilas Sarang (ed.), *Indian English Poetry* (Hyderabad: Disha Books, 1990), pp. 6−7.

18 In Meenakshi Sharma (ed.), *The Wordsmiths* (New Delhi: Katha Rupa & Co., 1996), p. 28.

19 Translated from the Tamil by the poet, in Vinay Dharwadker and A.K. Ramanujan (eds), *The Oxford Anthology of Modern Indian Poetry* (New Delhi: Oxford University Press, 1994), p. 101.

20 M.K. Naik, 'Echo and Voice in Indian Poetry in English', in idem (ed.),

Indian Responses to Poetry in English (Madras: Macmillan, 1970), p. 277.

21 M.K. Naik, 'The Achievement of Indian English Poetry', in idem, *Dimensions of Indian English Literature* (New Delhi: Sterling Publishers, 1984), p. 11.

22 M.K. Naik, 'The Indianness of Indian Poetry in English', *Journal of Indian Writing in English* 1.2, July 1973, p. 7.

23 R. Parthasarathy, 'Whoring After English Gods', in S.P. Bhagat (ed.), *Perspectives* (Bombay: Popular Prakashan, 1970), p. 57.

24 R. Parthasarathy, 'Indian English Verse: The Making of a Tradition', in Avadesh K Srivastava (ed.), *Alien Voice* (Lucknow: Print House, 1981), p. 44, original emphasis.

25 Eunice de Souza, 'The Critic in a Post-Colonial Situation with Reference to Indian Poetry in English', unpublished doctoral thesis, University of Bombay, 1987, p. 155.

26 De Souza, 'The Critic in a Post-Colonial Situation', p. 143.

27 De Souza, 'The Critic in a Post-Colonial Situation', pp. 132–3.

28 Gieve Patel, *How Do You Withstand, Body* (Bombay: Clearing House, 1976), p. 26.

29 M.R. Satanarayana in Vasant A. Shahane and M. Sivaramkrishna (eds), *Indian Poetry in English* (Delhi: Macmillan, 1980), p. 72.

30 Satanarayana on *Jejuri*, in Shahane and Sivaramkrishna (eds), *Indian Poetry in English*, p. 72.

31 Satanarayana on *Jejuri*, in Shahane and Sivaramkrishna (eds), *Indian Poetry in English*, p. 73.

32 De Souza, 'The Critic in a Post-Colonial Situation', p. 162.

33 Quoted in 'What is an Indian Poem?' *Fulcrum* 4, 2005, p. 513.

34 'What is an Indian Poem?', p. 514.

35 'What is an Indian Poem?', p. 515.

36 'What is an Indian Poem?', p. 515.

37 G.J.V. Prasad, 'Desperately Seeking India', in idem, *In Delhi Without a Visa* (New Delhi: Har-Anand Publications, 1996), p. 18.

Death Matters: Intimacy, Violence and the Production of Social Knowledge by Urban Youth in the Democratic Republic of Congo

FILIP DE BOECK

My contribution will deal with our ultimate but intimate, internal Other, the other that is constantly with us and punctuates the line of our lives: Death. In Kinshasa, the capital of the Democratic Republic of Congo, death and the way in which it is managed by urban youth has generated radically new geographies of proximity and distance, of inclusion and exclusion between Kinois youth and their elders. The growing cultural rift between young and old, and the ongoing efforts at rephrasing existing notions of gerontocracy and authority that accompany these new fractures, are also played out along other vault lines, such as between public and private, modernity and tradition, politics and morality, between those who have a right to the city and those who do not, or between conflicting notions of citizenship and law. My ethnography of youth's dealings with death, therefore, highlights ongoing efforts to reconceptualise the use of public urban space, the meaning of the public sphere, the content of citizenship, and the efforts of urban youth to generate a new moral ground from which to formulate alternatives to official ideologies as defined within the frameworks of State and Church.

Prelude

As a kid, I loved to visit my maternal grandparents' house in Hoboken, an Antwerp suburb. Their apartment occupied two floors of a large house that also contained my grandfather's business, a family business he had inherited from his father, and which he passed on to my maternal uncle, who in turn left it in the hands of his own son, one of my maternal cousins.

At the time, the nature of my grandfather's business did not strike me in the least as being special or odd. My grandfather was a well-established undertaker, and dealt with the dead on a daily basis. Yet, my grandparents' house constantly bristled with life. Its nerve centre was an office where the deceased's red-eyed family members, dressed in their Sunday best in black mourning-suits smelling of mothballs, were offered a cup of coffee, and discussed the practical organisation of the funeral with my grandmother in subdued and formal voices. Next to the office was a smaller room filled with the smell of lead and ink, where the printer and his apprentice composed mourning-cards on a medieval-looking printing press. In an adjacent room funeral wreaths were made from plastic or silk flowers, while yet another room was used to store the drapes for the chapels and the costumes of the chauffeurs and bearers. In the huge garage at the back of the building the horses and funeral coaches of a previous generation had been replaced by the smell of motor oil and rubber. Ten 'corbillards', luxurious silver-grey and black Cadillac funeral cars which my grandfather had proudly imported from the USA, were maintained by a whole crew of car mechanics. In the basement, which smelled of wood, sawdust and varnish, carpenters made the coffins in which my brother and I would play hide-and-seek once they were lined up along the basement's walls. Finally, there was one room we were denied access to, but which occupied an important place in our imagination: death's own beauty parlour, with one cold blue steel wall of refrigerators, in which the bodies of the deceased silently awaited their burial or incineration (although cremation was still considered a rather objectionable practice by many in the Catholic Flanders of the 1960s). All of this remained invisible to the visitors who came to pay their respects to their relative, friend or colleague, laid in state in the funeral parlour.

My grandfather's house, in short, contained a whole factory for the handling of dead bodies, a necropolis bristling with life, in which everyone contributed to a smooth, indeed almost Fordist, management of death in all of its different material aspects. What did not strike me then as anything out of the ordinary, but what I often wonder about today, is the intimate and matter-of-fact kind of way in which my grandparents lived and dealt with the dead, and how death itself was a constant – though never disturbing but on the contrary very familiar and reassuring – presence in their daily routines and conversations. I have vivid memories of how my grandfather (an imposing figure, always with a cigar in his mouth, and, in my memory at least, always dressed in a black tail-coat and high hat), upon coming home after a day's work, would seat himself at the head of the dinner table, put out his cigar, undo the shirt-button of his stiff white cardboard neckband, ask one of us to lead in prayer, and then, while putting some more salt in his soup (for soup was an integral part of every Flemish meal in those days), start to relate to my grandmother – and much to our excitement – whom he buried today, which body parts had to be picked up after someone had jumped under a train, how difficult it was to get the corpse of so-and-so dressed. And for a moment it seemed as if the deceased of that day were sitting with us around the table, feeling slightly out of their element in their best Sunday outfits, but politely listening to my grandfather's stories about them.

Introduction: Children of Disorder in the Cemetery State

Mokolo nakokufa nayebi te, ndenge bakolela nga. Na mbeto souci te, fête ya bato nionso. Kinshasa ekoma façon. Esika ya liwa ekoma fête. Bayeli nde mibali, mibali bayeli nde chéries. Mokolo nakokufa ekozala se bongo. Soki bameli balangwe, bayei kotutuka. Nani abomi ye? (I do not know the day I will die, nor do I know how they will mourn me. Stretched out on the bed, nothing to worry about any longer, it is party time for everybody. This has become the norm in Kinshasa. The place of death has become a place to party. The women come to find a man, and the men come for a girl. It will be like that on the day I die. And they will drink and get drunk, and then start brutalising everybody: 'Who killed this man?' [implied: by means of witchcraft])

Song by musician Lutumba Simaro

April 2008 – Kinshasa, the cemetery of Kintambo.[1] Although four decades separate me from my childhood, and although the cemetery setting is radically different, the connection with death immediately brings back memories of my grandfather's house. As I find myself walking on top of human remains, often hastily buried in this vast cemetery which is one of the city's oldest and also one of the fullest, the sickly smell of rotting corpses is undeniable. Whereas the dead at my grandfather's behaved politely and almost apologetically, as if they were embarrassed to interrupt the life of the living, here the dead brutally stare you in the face. Not only every coffin in Kinshasa has glass windows so that the corpse can at all times see and be seen, but death itself has become very unruly in Kinshasa.

The cemetery of Kintambo, once the main cemetery of Léopoldville, and in use since the 1930s at least, is literally overflowing with corpses. In the late 1980s already, the urban authorities closed this cemetery down, but today, after two more official closures, the inhabitants of the neighbouring *quartiers*, the populated slum areas of Camp Luka, Quartier Congo and the slightly more upscale Jamaïk, still continue to bury their dead there. Every day, more corpses arrive in this cemetery that has long been abandoned by the city's authorities.[2] No longer taken care of, the cemetery has become, in the words of the Kinois, 'a forest where snakes lay their eggs'. The original ground-plan of the cemetery has totally disappeared. It has made place for a lush vegetation that has totally overgrown this Thanatopolis, burying the dead for a second time. Here indeed, one dies twice: tombs and coffins are looted, or washed away by the rainy season's torrential storms, causing the dead bodies to disappear as rapidly as they were buried. Often, also, graves are recycled and different corpses are buried on top of each other owing to lack of space. Other tombs are destroyed to make place for illegal housing constructions, for in this urban jungle the living and the dead are engaged in a sometimes fierce competition over land. Walking along the main dust road cutting through this cemetery, I am reminded of my grandfather's intimate, doxic way of dealing with the dead. Here too, the living and the dead live in close proximity; their lives seem intimately related. Kids play football between eroded graves; tombstones along the road serve as shop windows for second-hand clothes, bottles of palm wine, or plastic vessels made in China, which vendors with loud voices try to sell to passers-by; women harvest the corn and groundnuts that grow from the bellies of the dead; mortuary houses inside the cemetery are used as shelters by street children (whom Kinois refer to as *société morte*, dead society), while gravediggers turn tombstones along the main road into their personal office spaces. In fact, through an informal commoditisation of death, the cemetery has become a market, a place to satisfy one's 'thirst for money' (*lokoso*). Youngsters offer their services to the family members of the deceased or to the gravediggers. The latter are organised in a 'stable' (*écurie*).[3]

More important, however, than the cemetery's decaying material infrastructure, or the seeming informalisation of death's economy that is performed on the graveyard's surface, is the fact that the management of death and the labour of loss is no longer controlled and performed by elders, but is increasingly in the hands of children and youngsters. Whereas before children and youngsters were physically barred and protected by their parents and elders from contact with the dead, they now seem to have developed the most intimate connection with death.

The presence of death has indeed profoundly reconfigured the access and use of public space in the urban setting. Some decades ago, in Kinshasa, placing the body of a deceased person in the middle of the street would have been unthinkable. In the 1960s and 1970s mourning rituals took place inside the compounds, while children and youngsters were barred from any contact with death itself. If a funeral procession passed through the street, mothers would call their children indoors: children were not supposed to come into contact with death, since they represent the beginning of life and should not be contaminated by its end. Today, however, owing to lack of space within the compounds, the body of the deceased is often placed upon a bier in the middle of the street, under a funeral chapel, and people gather around the body to mourn the deceased and hold nocturnal wakes accessible to all. Streets are blocked and palm leaves are placed at their entrance. As such, the dead, also because they have become so numerous, have quite literally taken possession of the urban public space and have redefined its meaning and its use in the process.

Today, children and youngsters have taken over the control of the mourning and burial rituals. They are also the ones to accompany the deceased on their last journey from the compound to the cemetery. This phenomenon might be observed throughout the city, but it is especially the case in Camp Luka, an overpopulated slum area which borders on the cemetery of Kintambo and which grew out of an illegal squatting area in the 1970s. Among its inhabitants Camp Luka is known as 'The State' (*Leta*). Camp Luka's youngsters, who call themselves the 'children of the State' (*bana Etat*) or 'the children of disorder' (*bana désordre*), impose disorder, their law, the unruly 'law' of this strange and ragged state, on to the cemetery and indeed the rest of the city. They do so in effervescent ways, ludic and violent at once, during the mourning rituals (*matanga*) and funerals, and through the materiality and aesthetics of the body – both their own and that of the dead.

My contribution is situated at the nexus between (corporeal) intimacy, violence and the production of social knowledge by urban youth in Congo. More specifically, I focus on the ways in which, in this urban site, the vitality of the youthful body and the 'life of the corpse' connect, to use the phrase by the Mexican artist Teresa Margolles.[4] Youth and death are two categories that normally exclude each other, but that have become intimately connected in Kinshasa. It is this connection that provokes us to think about the seemingly counterintuitive ways in which young people confronted with powerful societal problems articulate their 'law', their sociality, out of the very source of their desperation. By eliding life and death, by placing us in the presence of death, Kinois youth forcefully remove the distance we would normally place between ourselves and the dead, and give a new identity to themselves as well as to the city.

If, as Lévi-Strauss famously remarked in the concluding pages of *Tristes Tropiques*, cities are machines 'destinées à produire de l'inertie à un rhythme et dans une proportion infiniment plus élevée que la quantité d'organisation qu'ils impliquent', the cemetery of Kintambo seems indeed to be the right place to redefine anthropology as *entropology*, 'une discipline vouée à étudier dans ses manifestations les plus hautes ce processus de désintégration'.[5] But is this what is really going on in Kinshasa's burial grounds? It is easy to read a space such as the cemetery of Kintambo, with its infrastructural degradation and the breakdown of cultural norms and longstanding notions of social order that accompany this material decay, as a general metaphor for the zombified state of a city and a country that, in the words of Kinois, 'died' or 'rotted a long time ago' (*mboka ekufi, mboka ebebi*), or are conceived of as terminally ill and *cadavéré*.[6] But are notions of entropy, chaos, disorder or dissipation of energy adequate tools to understand the dynamics of a place such as the cemetery of Kintambo? Do they have sufficient explanatory power to fully capture the meanings embedded in the new mourning and funeral practices that have developed around it? It is indeed tempting, perhaps even too obvious, to understand Kinshasa's postcolonial cemetery as a mere zone of social abandonment, to use Biehl's term,[7] a zone of abandonment with specific Agamben-esque connotations, in which the law is in force but no longer has substantive meaning.[8] The cemetery of Kintambo and its surrounding slums indeed offer an almost camp-like infrastructure (as Camp Luka's name already indicates in itself) which exemplifies the state of exception that has become the rule in postcolonial Congo. This abandonment illustrates to what extent Kinois are turned into *homines sacri*, collectively reduced to the specific forms of *vie nue*, the raw bare life as described by Agamben, that is, a politicised form of natural life, a life exposed and subjugated to death, placed outside both the divine and the profane law.

In this contribution, however, my focus of attention is not so much on the processes of zombification that seem to pervade both the *cité cimetière*, the cemetery city, that Kinshasa (as well as the 'thanatocracy' called Congo) has become. Rather, I want to analyse how youngsters, through their cohabitation with death and the generation of new forms of mourning and coping with dispersal and loss, reframe the conditions of such bare life into something else. Through an ethnographic description of their – sometimes violent – involvement in matters pertaining to death, I will analyse specific local attempts made by Kinshasa's youth to turn the aporia of this naked life form into more euphoric solutions. In the process, I argue, urban youngsters reconceptualise the camp, the very territory of death itself, in terms of a more heterotopic space. This effort enables Kinois youth to contest and rethink the time of the state and the postcolonial political order, and in so doing express their longing for new political futures.[9] It also offers them the possibility to redefine Congo's ongoing economic and socio-political crisis in terms of a primarily *moral* critique of the specific necropolitics that underpins the postcolonial state of exception.[10]

Youth, Religion and Death in the Apocalyptic Interlude

For decades now, Congo has been in the grip of a profound crisis, which makes itself felt in every field and on every level of Congolese society: politically, economically, socially and culturally.[11] In fact, the crisis is experienced to be so multiform and omnipresent that there hardly seems to be a way out of the harsh living conditions it has created. 'We live like animals' (Lingala: *tokomi kovivre lokola banyama*) is an often-heard remark in Kinshasa's streets. One of the only available answers to face the hardships imposed by this widespread crisis is provided by religion. Over the past two decades, as elsewhere in Congo and indeed Africa, Kinshasa has witnessed the rapid spread of Christian fundamentalist churches. Replacing to an important extent the 'traditional' Catholic and Protestant religious practices that were introduced during colonial times, Pentecostalism, churches of awakening, charismatic renewal churches and other millenarian movements have deeply penetrated the lives of city dwellers. It is this Christian fundamentalism that has imposed its logic and its temporality onto the city. This temporality is of a very specific eschatological kind and takes its point of departure in the Bible, and more particularly in the book of Revelation, which has become the omnipresent point of reference in Kinshasa's collective imagination. The lived-in time of daily life in Kinshasa is constantly projected against the canvas of the completion of everything, a completion which will be brought about by God. As such, Kinshasa is captured in 'the apocalyptic interlude',[12] a moment that has also profoundly changed the meaning and the emplacement of death in the religious realm.[13]

However, the very field of death, and the practices that are generated around it, seem to escape, at least to some extent, the hegemony and control of the churches, whether of Pentecostalist signature or orthodox Catholic or Protestant. The funeral processions that accompany the deceased to his or her last resting place in the cemetery have often turned into moments of contestation of existing, religious as well as political, figures and structures of authority. When the coffin with the corpse is carried through the streets, especially if the deceased was a young person, children and youth flock around it to sing songs with an outspoken political character: *Toyei, toyei matanga, toboyi baconseillers, soki olingi koteya, teya bandimi na yo. Soki olingi koteya teya bana na yo. Soki olingi koteya teya na ndako na yo* (We go, we go to the mourning ritual. We refuse the councillors – the elders' authority. If you want to preach, preach for your believers. If you want to preach, preach for your own children. If you want to preach, preach in your own house). Other songs have a clearly political content: *Bana na diplome bakei koteka mayi, bana na diplome bakeyi koteka boudin. Pays riche lokumu ezali wapi?* (Children with a diploma sell water, children with a diploma sell sausages. A rich country, but where is dignity?). Sometimes they even give voice to a nostalgia for the former Mobutist regime: *Mobutu Mobutu tango okenda loso na loso* (Mobutu ever since you left, we only eat rice [we are hungry]).

Funerals, however, have become much more than moments of

contestation for a rebellious urban youth. Their social and political criticism reaches far beyond the level of official state politics, and touches on deeply moral issues, related to much more intimate domains. Their actions pose fundamental questions with regard to the possibility of intersubjective relations; possible reconfigurations of what kinship might mean and of the dividing lines between insider and stranger; or the very definition of the notion of ancestrality, and the feasibility of continued intergenerational transmission of social knowledge. All of this comes to the surface during the *matanga*, the mourning rituals that accompany the death and burial of a parent, a beloved one, a friend or a neighbour.

Youth, Death and Witchcraft Accusations in the Urban Public Realm

Matanga have always been extremely important communal moments of encounter, creating wide-ranging social networks that are regenerated from one *matanga* to the next. As Durham and Klaits remark with regard to funerals in Botswana, 'people find themselves connected in their very physical well-being through emotional states and sentimental connections recognized and forged in public space'.[14] What produces the connectedness between all those present is the sense of shared, collective *Trauer Arbeit*, shaping up around an intimate, often corporeal and tactile, and always highly emotional relationship with the very body of the deceased. Family members, friends and neighbours gather around the dead body, weep, sing, address the deceased, touch and embrace the body, dance around it and take care of it during a whole night of mourning, until its burial the next day. That does not exclude this collective labour of loss from being a ludic happening as well. *Matanga* invariably also offer occasions for laughter, amusement, flirting and excitement; they hold out the promise of new encounters, or the joy of meeting up with old friends and acquaintances. At the same time, *matanga* are very weighty occasions in which existing hierarchies and power relations within and between families, lineages and clans are reaffirmed or contested. Usually, the maternal uncles of the deceased are the ones in charge of the funeral. They decide upon the time and place of burial, raise the necessary money, hire chairs, an orchestra and/or choir, contact the authorities, take care of the formalities for burial, meet the cemetery authorities, supervise the unfolding of the mourning period until the burial, assemble the deceased's family (the mother's and father's side, and the in-laws), conduct the palavers surrounding heritage and funeral contributions, and, most importantly, establish the cause of death, certainly in cases where witchcraft is suspected to be at the origin of a person's death.

In Kinshasa today, *matanga* often continue to be important motors for the production and renewal of the cohesion of social networks, especially if the deceased is an adult person or elder. The *matanga* is the nocturnal time-space in which the whole social landscape that unfolds between people during the day is constructed. It sets the scene for the replenishing of the social weave which unfolds during the day.

Matanga lose their broader integrative force, however, when a young person dies. In that case, suspicions about witchcraft are quick to surge to the surface. Youngsters in particular are quick to blame the deceased's parents, uncles and elders for this death (*balei ye, babomi ye*; they ate him, they killed him). Usually, such accusations tend to drastically alter the course of the funeral itself. The *matanga* almost invariably 'turns into disorder' (*matanga ekomi désordre, pito-pale*) and becomes an intergenerational battlefield. When that happens, the deceased's friends, his or her classmates, or just any youngster living in the same neighbourhood, are likely to take over the control of the *matanga* and of the funeral rituals. These groups of youngsters, the 'people of disorder' (*bato ya désordre*), sometimes in collaboration with local youth gangs, referred to as the 'strong people' (*bato ya makassi*) or *yanke* (from 'yankee'), often start to throw stones at all who are present on the site of mourning.[15] They uproot the trees in the compound, or attack the deceased's parental home, often destroying or burning it down in the process, while beating up or chasing away the parents, uncles, aunts and preachers who are gathered there to mourn the deceased. The general atmosphere quickly turns into a chaotic and often violent mood, further enhanced by the young-sters' singing and dancing (in ways inspired by South African toy-toying), and the lavish use of marijuana and locally brewed alcohol (*lungwuila*, *chichampa* or *lotoko*). Invading the scene of mourning they will single out certain elders while singing: *Tango mosusu ndoki ye yo ye yo* (Maybe the witch is this one or that one). The youngsters will then confiscate the abandoned dead body, block the street and erect a 'frontier' (*barrière*). In this way they 'colonise' public space to establish their 'state', their 'rule', which is marked by the order of disorder.[16] They force passers-by to make a monetary contribution. In case they refuse, they risk, at the very least, being dirtied with a mixture of burned rubber and palm oil. The money thus extracted is often spent on the burial itself.

Clearly, at that point, the deceased's family members no longer control the funeral, and do not risk showing up at the funeral itself. Frequently, it is only after completion of the burial that the respon-sibility for the dead person is handed over again to his or her family, and not without long negotiations over whom the *muziku*, the money raised by the *matanga*'s participants, should go to. Sometimes the family of the deceased tries to mobilise the police to regain control over the corpse during the funeral procedures, but often the policemen refuse to get involved. And when they do, their intervention often leads to a further deterioration of the situ-ation. Not infrequently, youngsters are hit by police bullets on such occasions.

Under these circumstances, the funeral itself inevitably turns into a highly chaotic event. Minibuses and cars are routinely confis-cated in the street by youths. Sitting on the car's rooftop or hanging out of the windows while singing and shouting, they use these hijacked cars to drive to the cemetery at high speed. Often the coffin with the corpse is paraded through the streets, carried by the deceased's friends and surrounded by dancing boys and girls singing lewd songs, full of sexual license, while revealing certain body parts and making obscene gestures: *Lelo libola etuli, lelo libola ekei kopola* (Today the vagina no longer works, today the vagina will rot away). Other songs include: *Awa ezali hotel. Oyei, osali, ya premier coup ezalaka direct* (Here [the cemetery] it is a hotel. You come, you make love, and from the very first shot it is goal!) or *Mayi! Mayi! Mayi mibali, mayi mayi mikongo, mayi mayi! Soki nakangi yo nakocha yo etsubeli, etsubeli, etsubeli! Nakosiba yo!* (Water, men's water, water from the backbone [sperm], water, water! When I catch you, I will put my penis inside you, the penis, the penis, I will fuck you!).

Often, also, during these unruly funeral processions, the young carriers of the body perform a divinatory ritual on the corpse, asking the dead person to direct them to those responsible for his death (namely his family elders).

The same frenzied atmosphere characterises the burial itself. Here youngsters often start to dance on the graves, while undressing and exposing their genital parts (*mutakala, nzoto libanda*).

Youth and the Resacralisation of Death

At first glance, death seems to have become a banal reality in the urban context, when compared to the elaborate funeral rituals and mortuary prescriptions that existed in the rural hinterland surrounding Kinshasa until recently.[17] Youngsters will no longer use the more respectful Lingala word *kufa*, to die, but will speak instead of *dayé* (from the English 'to die'), to show their indifference or even disdain for death. This seeming banalisation, and according to many older Kinois, even desecration of death, expresses itself in various ways: not only in the language youngsters use to denote death, but also in the general attitude towards the dead, who no longer inspire fear, awe and respect, or in the mere fact that the dividing line between the living and the dead has become so difficult to trace. As Kinois say: 'We (the living and the dead) are all the same' (*biso nionso bato moko*). For most youngsters, and in spite of the influence of Pentecostalism, death signifies the end. There is nothing beyond death, one just disappears. This attitude sharply contrasts with former autochthonous beliefs in ancestrality. Today, however, it seems as if the production of ancestors, at least in the mind of these youngsters, has ground to a standstill. No longer the prerogative of elders, the management of death is used by the young to contest the authority of ancestors, and by extension, adults: 'If you do not watch out,' they threaten their elders, 'we will make you eat the shovel' (*okoliya mpau*), meaning: we will bury you. 'How can we still respect the elders?' youngsters told me.

> They are the ones who should uphold tradition, who tell us about the important place of the ancestors, but when you see how they cope with the dead who will become the ancestors, when you observe how their corpses are put in the street, how they are buried hastily, how can you continue to believe this? Our elders have turned the process of dying into a *fait-divers*, and they have started to treat the dead with disrespect. So why should we still respect the elders?

Funerals, in this way, have not only become a means for political contestation, but in a much broader sense death has become an occasion for youngsters to criticise the role of parents and elders who have *démissioné*, who have given up, who no longer seem to be able to fulfil their promises, and whose moral authority has vanished. In the light of this failure of gerontocracy, 'corpses have become the responsibility of the youngsters of the neighbourhood' (*bibembe ekoma ya bana quartier*). The dead have become their 'toy' (*eloko ya jeu*), and the coffin, so this urban youth claims, has become like a football that one tosses up and plays with. Youngsters, in short, have become 'the directors' (*bazali kodiriger*) and have taken over the control of the dead, while elders 'have become little children' (*bakomi bana mike*).

These are radical societal shifts, which accompany a disturbing demographic reality: Not only is death and its management no longer the prerogative of elders, they are also no longer the only ones to die. Life expectancy in Congo is among the globe's lowest, and the young die in great numbers. The intimate connection between youth and death provokes us to think differently about the seemingly counterintuitive ways in which young people in Kinshasa confronted with powerful problems articulate a semblance of sociality out of the very source of their desperation. In fact, what appears to be a desecralisation and banalisation of death by youngsters hides a totally different register. In the face of economic ruin, homelessness, apocalyptic predictions, and baseless hopes, young Kinois have designed a new architecture of urban survival for which death, and the very materiality and aesthetics of the dead body, by seeping so visibly and violently into the fabric of life, now serves as an inspirational force, a structural support, a framing device for negotiating social relationships and constructing identities. In a world where mourning has reconfigured meaning, where cemeteries have become dwellings for the living, and where coffins are likened to the footballs that boys toss around, the only way to live is to manage death. For young Kinois who deal with dead bodies on a routine basis, dying is no longer a departure from life, it has become that which gives life its significance, density and directionality. Life, in fact, cannot be lived, nor spoken, nor even imagined outside of the space of death.

Conclusion: Youth, the Morality of Disorder and the Ethics of Being Human

The repositioning of death enables youngsters in Kinshasa to break away from older models and to redraw the social and moral landscapes of urban public life. Firstly, funerals offer the possibility of rejecting current official political and religious order (all the more surprising given the thorough grasp of the millennial churches on all other aspects of public life in Congo today). Secondly, funerals form key moments to contest the role of the elders, who are perceived to have abandoned their responsibilities and have failed to live up to the expectations of the young they are supposed to guide and protect. Mourning rituals and funerals thus bear witness to the profound crisis of intergenerational transmission and of existing structures of family and kinship. Funerals, in their guise of ritualised moments of rebellion against the established order, allow youngsters to design an alternative political and also moral landscape. By replacing the rule of the state, the church, the ancestor and the elder with their own rule, which is characterised by 'disorder', young Kinois reshape the city's outlook and draw an alternative cartography of the urban public sphere. They abandon older prescriptions, taboos, norms and forms surrounding death and mourning and are thus perceived by the generations of their parents and grandparents as sacrificers of the sacred, as desecrators of the dead, and therefore as highly immoral actors in an urban universe that is otherwise characterised by the high moral discourses of Pentecostalism.

Paradoxically, though, the same young urban actors reintroduce other aspects of much older, pre-urban ritual dynamics, in an 'enactment of moral sentiment'.[18] The lewd songs and insults which were mentioned above, the exposure of body parts, the whole play with the body's surface and its politics of undress[19] are very 'heterotopian', in that they constitute a Turnerian anti-structural moment of ritual reversal quite common in a number of Central African rituals.[20] In this sense, also, one should understand the way in which youngsters ritually ridicule death and disease, by performing dances in front of the corpse of their dead friend, by imitating physically impaired people, thereby keeping death, disease and misfortune itself at bay. Another way in which tradition is recycled, for example, is through the performance of dances such as *musangu*, a dance traditionally only performed by Lunda and Yaka elders on important political occasions. In the urban context this dance is performed by the young friends of the deceased as a form to salute and praise him.

In various ways, then, Kinois youngsters shape a future for more traditional ritual forms, of which they often do not even have first-hand knowledge, but which they nonetheless reinvent single-handedly in the urban context. Against the order of the State and the Church, with their promotion of what essentially remains a very colonialist modernity, urban youth introduces its own moralities, while rejecting the moral codes of Church and State and the modernity they promote. In using the body of the dead as an alternative political platform to speak out, they introduce their own bodies as tools for self-making and for exercising their critique against older forms of authority. In this they seem to exemplify what Bogumil Jewsiewicki and Bob White write in their introduction to a special issue of *African Studies Review* on 'mourning' in Central Africa: 'As death seems increasingly present in the lives of people in many parts of Africa, emerging forms of social mourning echo the need for new political futures, and mourning shows itself as an important terrain for the social production of meaning.'[21]

Kinois youth's criticism, though, transcends the mere political level. Theirs is essentially a moral criticism of the world they live in. The outside, the urban public sphere, is criticised, reshaped by positing it against its opposite: the intimate corporeal space of inner self and intersubjective relations. Through a discourse and songs that refer to love making, sexuality and play, and by means of a powerful and transgressive act of symbolic copulation between two bodies, that is, the strong and youthful body and the corpse, with all of its rotting, disintegrating, dissolving, smelly immediacy, youngsters shout this basic question to Kinois society as a whole: what does it mean to be human in the light of the constant threat of sudden disappearance and annihilation, in a context of systematic abandon and generalised, material as well as spiritual, insecurity?

Against the omnipresence of death, and the constant threat of being annihilated and forgotten, the corporeal dimension of juvenile vocabularies of self-realisation powerfully posits the city in the immediate time frame of the moment, the now, to celebrate its vitality and life and to offer an alternative to this degradation. This urban life saturated with deadness, which numbs everything and everyone, stands paradoxically against what is shown as the generative dimension of death, that is, the power that death has not simply to mortify life but in fact to *enliven* it. At the same time, the strange cartel between youth and death forces the city to stare into the face of its own death, and thereby into the darkest corners of its own modalities of existence. Juvenile bodies, whether dead or alive, here appear as lucid, ludic but also subversive sites and frontiers of re-territorialisation, not only of official cultural and political programmes, but also of the much deeper and darker sides of what constitutes humanity in this urban setting. They struggle to redefine the *vie nue*, with all of the horror and disgust that come with it, and reanimate this bare life with new forms of profane and divine law. That is also the new meaning of the graveyard. It provides urban youth with a heterotopic space to express the crisis, and to find forms to both *embody* and overcome the disintegration of their state, their city, their society and its moral values.

Notes

1 My ethnography builds on several years of field research in the city of Kinshasa. Research in Congo was made possible by a number of grants from the Flemish Fund for Scientific Research (FWO-Vlaanderen) as well as by a grant from the Flemish Community to develop an exhibition project entitled 'Kinshasa, the imaginary city' (cf. F. De Boeck and M.-F. Plissart, *Kinshasa: Tales of the Invisible City* [Ghent: Ludion; Tervuren: Royal Museum for Central Africa, 2004]). More recently, for several months between 2005 and 2008, I carried out research in a number of cemeteries in Kinshasa. Most of this field research was conducted in the cemetery of Kintambo, which is located between two of Kinshasa's more popular, populous and poor neighbourhoods: Camp Luka, a neighbourhood in the commune of Ngaliema, and Jamaik, part of Kintambo, one of Kinshasa's oldest communes (see F. De Boeck, '"Dead Society" in a "Cemetery City": The Transformation of Burial Rites in Kinshasa', in L. Decauter and M. Dehaene [eds], *Heterotopia and the City: Public Space in a Postcivil Society* [London: Routledge, 2008]). Other cemeteries in Kinshasa and its periphery include Kimbanseke and Gombe (named after the commune where they are located), Kinsuka and Kimwenza (both in the commune of Mont Ngafula), Mbenseke and Mitendi (on the road to Matadi and the Lower Congo), Kisenzo (on the border between the communes of Mont Ngafula and Kisenzo), Kingampio, CIFORCO (ex-CIFORZAL) (in Masina, near the international airport), Mikonga (on the road towards Maluku), Kinkole (in the commune of Nsele) and Gombe Lutete. Some of these cemeteries were opened by the (post)colonial authorities, others were originally traditional burial grounds of the Teke-Humbu, the local landowners and original inhabitants of Kinshasa (such as the cemeteries of Kingampio, Kimwenza, Mikonga and Sans Fil in Masina). Some cemeteries such as Kanza, Sans Fil and Makala have ceased to exist in the meantime, while others are

menaced by the uncontrolled and rapid urban sprawl (Kinsuka, Kisenso). Some cemeteries are also threatened by erosions (Kisenso) or were officially closed by the authorities (as in the case of Kasavubu, where the cemetery subsequently became a huge vegetable garden). Finally, numerous burial sites in and around the city of Kinshasa are not known to the city's authorities.

2 A lot of burials are still taking place at the cemetery of Kintambo. At the *Division Urbaine* of Kinshasa, the city's administrative unit responsible for all of Kinshasa's cemeteries, no official statistics are kept about the number of burials performed every year throughout the city. However, since 2002, the new head of the *Service d'Inhumation* keeps track himself of the number of burials, and arrives at a yearly average of 21,968 deaths (until 2005). The cemetery of Tsuengu (Masina SIFORCO) seems to absorb more bodies than any other cemetery, but Kintambo still ranks second, with 25.17 per cent of the city's burials in 2002, 24.31 per cent in 2003 and 21.47 per cent in 2004. That means that 23.65 per cent of all of Kinshasa's deceased for these years was buried in a cemetery that no longer exists officially. (I have only received figures for the first nine months of 2005, and none for later years.)

3 In the cemetery of Kintambo the main 'stable' is called *Shamukwale*, the name of a village near the Angolan border. At this location people enter into Angola, in order to engage in clandestine artisanal diamond mining. Grave-digging is here compared, not without irony, to diamond digging. The *Ecurie Shamukwale*, an informal overarching association, consists of a number of separate smaller groups, such as the *Ecurie Bana Cimetière, Ecurie Etat-Major* or *Camp Kawele, Ecurie Camp PM* (Military Police), *Ecurie Camp Police*, etc. The person recognised by most as the head of the informal Shamukwale association is the older brother of one of the cemetery administrative officials, who reside under the city governor's authority. These officials are supposed to register the dead and collect certain taxes.

The members of the informal gravedigger groups are all young boys and men from the surrounding neighbourhoods. Other youngsters who offer informal services in and around the cemetery are often also organised in similar *écurie* structures. These various groups at the cemetery of Kintambo offer specific services (digging graves, fabricating crosses, maintaining the tombs, and so forth). Some of these youngsters also offer their services for clandestine burials. Very often, people who cannot afford to finance a burial are forced to bury their dead in a secret and non-official way. This happens more frequently when the deceased is a young child. Along the dust road which cuts through the cemetery and forms the access to the neighbourhood of Camp Luka, a small group of male adolescents, members of the *Ecurie Tshico*, wait to be contacted by parents who want to bury their child without registering with the authorities and bypassing the regular formalities. In such a case the burial is carried out at nightfall. Other groups of youngsters spend their days waiting along the cemetery to be hired as singers and drummers during the funeral. Others still await nightfall to dig up and steal the coffins of those who were buried during the day. These coffins are subsequently resold (cf. De Boeck and Plissart, *Kinshasa*, p. 136). Finally, some youngsters await the night to pillage the graves in the hope of laying their hands on clothes and jewellery.

4 U. Kittelmann and K. Gorner (eds), *Teresa Margolles: Muerte Sin Fin* (Ostfildern-Ruit: Hatje Cantz, 2004).

5 C. Lévi-Strauss, *Tristes tropiques* (Paris: Plon, 1955), p. 478.

6 See Filip De Boeck, 'Beyond the Grave: History, Memory and Death in Postcolonial Congo/Zaire', in R. Werbner (ed.), *Memory and the Postcolony: African Anthropology and the Critique of Power* (London: Zed Books, 1998); De Boeck, 'The Apocalyptic Interlude: Revealing Death in Kinshasa', *African Studies Review* 48.2, 2005, pp. 11–32.

7 J. Biehl, *Vita: Life in a Zone of Social Abandonment* (Berkeley, CA: University of California Press, 2005).

8 G. Agamben, *State of Exception* (Chicago: University of Chicago Press, 2005).

9 B. Jewsiewicki and B. White, 'Introduction', *African Studies Review* 48.2, 2005, pp. 1–9. [Special issue on Mourning and the Imagination of Political Time in Contemporary Central Africa].

10 A. Mbembe, 'Necropolitics', *Public Culture* 15.1, 2003, pp. 11–40.

11 T. Trefon (ed.), *Reinventing Order in the Congo: How People Respond to State Failure in Kinshasa* (London: Zed Books, 2004).

12 De Boeck, 'The Apocalyptic Interlude'.

13 Elsewhere, I have described how death has become the general model for collective social and political action. De Boeck, 'Beyond the Grave'; De Boeck and Plissart, *Kinshasa*. See also I. Vangu Ngimbi, *Jeunesse, funérailles et contestation socio-politique en Afrique* (Paris: L'Harmattan, 1997).

14 D. Durham and F. Klaits, 'Funerals and the Public Space of Sentiment in Botswana', *Journal of Southern African Studies* 28.4, 2002, pp. 777–96 (778).

15 See also K. Geenen, '"Sleep Occupies no Space": The Use of Public Space by Street Gangs in Kinshasa', *Africa* (Journal of the Royal Anthropological Institute), in press; K. Pype, 'Fighting Boys, Strong Men, and Gorillas: Notes on the Imagination of Masculinities in Postcolonial Kinshasa (DR Congo)', *Africa* (Journal of the International Africa Institute) 77.2, 2007, pp. 250–71.

16 This phenomenon, which some Kinois interpret as a privatisation of the *matanga* as public event, is known as *kuluna*, a word derived from the Lingala verb *kolona*: to plant, to sow, to cultivate. The verb is, of course, itself a derivative of the French *coloniser*. In this way, youth's unruly law constitutes a particular example of the coincidence of disorder with the fixation on the legal that characterises postcolonial realities (cf. J. Comaroff and J. Comaroff [eds], *Law and Disorder in the Postcolony* [Chicago: University of Chicago Press, 2006]).

17 Cf. R. Devisch and W. de Mahieu, *Mort, Deuil et compensations mortuaires chez les Komo et les Yaka du nord au Zaïre* (Tervuren: Royal Museum for Central Africa, 1979).

18 J. Livingston, 'Disgust, Bodily Aesthetics and the Ethics of Being Human', *Africa* (Journal of the International African Institute) 78.2, 2008, pp. 288–307 (293).

19 Cf. Adeline Masquelier (ed.), *Dirt, Undress and Difference: Critical Perspectives on the Body's Surface* (Bloomington, IN: Indiana University Press, 2005).

20 See V. Turner, *The Ritual Process: Structure and Anti-Structure* (Ithaca, NY: Cornell University Press, 1969). Cf. Masquelier (ed.), *Dirt, Undress and Difference*.

21 Jewsiewicki and White, 'Introduction', p. 1.

Difference and Similarity:
The Burden of Identity

JORGE VALA

When the Portuguese arrived in Japan, around the mid-sixteenth century, they were amazed at the differences between Portuguese and Japanese customs, and as soon as 1583, Luís Fróis, a Portuguese Jesuit, published a work describing those differences. Most of these are described as *pure differences*: 'our food is bread, theirs is boiled rice with no salt', 'our churches are long and narrow, Japan's temples are wide and short'. Some differences, however, are presented in an evaluative and ethnocentric way: 'Our hair is pretty; Japanese's hair is clearly inferior', 'among us, betrayal is rare and punished; in Japan betrayal is common and surprises no one'.

Though carried out with mitigated ethnocentrism, Luís Fróis's descriptions are, however, more marked by contrast than by difference; that is, these are differences among equals. Or, as Lévi-Strauss wrote in the preface to the French edition of Fróis's book, the descriptions of this author are characterised by a search for symmetry between the two cultures, thus acknowledging them as different though equivalent. Lévi-Strauss goes on, saying: 'when the traveller realises that customs that are totally opposite to theirs, and which he would be tempted to negatively evaluate and reject, are identical to theirs when seen in a reverse way, he gives himself the possibility to control the strange and turn it into something familiar'.

Nonetheless, difference can equally play a fundamental role in processes of domination and exclusion, when its attribution takes place in a context of social relations between 'unequals'. We, therefore, face a polysemic concept. This polysemy is determined by the nature of social relations between the groups involved in the attribution of similarities and differences. Difference between equals is related with the idea of diversity and can be celebrated as a value. The attribution of differences between 'unequals' may be in itself a factor accentuating inequality and inferiorisation.

In this paper, we propose some reflections about the social construction of the meaning of cultural difference (and similarity) between unequals, and about its predictors and consequences. We analytically distinguish between two processes of dealing with the experience of difference. The first process refers to the attribution of cultural difference between human groups and relates to the following question: can the attribution of difference be an expression of inferiorisation? The second process refers to the reaction towards reified difference (and similarity) and relates to this other question: can socially objectified differences and similarities serve as the source of antagonistic relations between social groups?

The analysis of these processes and the answers to these questions will build on basic principles of a cognitive, motivational and ideological nature that organise collective thought on the relations between groups and communities. Among those principles, we underline the role of collective and individual identity.[1]

The Attribution of Difference as a Process of Inferiorisation

In recent years, we have developed a line of research that has theorised and has looked for empirical support to the hypothesis that the attribution of cultural differences between groups is, in many situations, a hidden form of inferiorisation of the Other. The meaning of this process is relevant, specifically in the context of social relations between majority groups and groups to which a different and inferior race has been attributed in the past. This process of conceiving the Other as different is a dynamic process moving between ethnocentrism and radical alterity.

In ethnocentrism, the Other is depicted as different and as having less value in a universe of common attributes. Radical alterity, as we see it, consists of describing the Other as radically different, as an entity that does not share any fundamental characteristic with us. In ethnocentrism, one witnesses a glorification of one's own group; in the process of radical alterity, what takes place is an inferiorisation and a derogation of the other group that can go as far as its exclusion from humankind. An example of the construction of the Other as radically different is provided by Edward Said in his widely known work, *Orientalism*.

The empirical investigation of prejudice, and specifically of racial prejudice, also offers diverse examples of radical alterity associated with the attribution of differences as a process of inferiorisation. For example, in the years following World War II, a large number of research projects showed that prejudiced people, specifically anti-Semites, when asked to categorise pictures of Jews and non-Jews, would categorise more non-Jews as Jews than would non anti-Semitic people. This means that the anti-Semites would make more errors of exclusion than inclusion in their 'ingroup'. Or stating it differently, prejudiced people were more sensitive to possible differences than non-prejudiced people, indicating their readiness to exclude others from their social world.

Furthermore, our own work has shown that the simple attribution of cultural difference to the Other – implicitly and subtly conceiving him as part of another culture or another ethnic group, a process that we termed as *hetero-ethnicisation* – is strongly related with prejudice, with traditional racist beliefs and with the orientation to discriminate against those to whom differences are attributed.

In the same vein, studies conducted by Serge Moscovici and other researchers have shown that in everyday language, an implicit difference is established between personality traits that we can call 'cultural', especially typical of humans (e.g. liar, wise), and traits that we can call 'natural' (e.g. friendly, noisy), common to humans and animals. The work of this author shows that, independently of their negativity or positivity, natural traits are more applied to groups that have been targets of explicit racialisation, like blacks and gipsies, than to our own group. The different Other is thus depicted as closer to nature and the animal world than to culture.

This phenomenon was equally studied by us and other colleagues in Switzerland. We asked respondents (German-speaking Swiss) to describe Swiss and other groups (Germans, eastern immigrants, Muslims and Africans) based on a list of adjectives, all positive, where half of them were related with 'nature' and the other half with 'culture'. Results showed that the description of other groups is made through the attribution of differences between our group and those groups; and those differences build on the attribution of more natural traits and less cultural traits to the other groups than to our own. Furthermore, one of those groups, the black Africans, was clearly inferiorised, being the only group to which the respondents attributed more natural than cultural traits. In another set of studies, Jacques Phillipe Leyens, together with other researchers, showed that in everyday life people implicitly distinguish between primary emotions and secondary emotions (or feelings), construing feelings (e.g. melancholy, compassion) as more characterising of humans, while primary emotions (e.g. fear, rage, joy) are seen as equally characteristic of humans and animals. In those same studies, it has been shown that, when people were asked to characterise their ingroup and the other groups (outgroups), they would attribute strong differences between them, recognising a larger capacity to express secondary emotions among their ingroup than the outgroups. The same does not happen with primary emotions, meaning that we are all animals, but some of us are more human than others.

An important aspect to retain from these studies is the fact that these call our attention to the important distinction between evaluation and inferiorisation within the realm of the subtle character that prejudice, racism and processes of alterity in general possess today. In this sense, a group may be evaluated positively in a series of traits and be, at the same time, considered inferior concerning an implicit pattern of humanity. For example, in the case of the attribution of personal characteristics, the use of positive words that nonetheless convey an image that is closer to nature than to culture constitutes a form of inferiorisation. The same can be said at the emotional level. In common sense, the ability to express primary positive emotions is not, in itself, a sign of humanity. Those who express more secondary emotions (feelings) are the ones who are considered humans, even if those emotions are negative. The distinction between hostile and benevolent sexism can also account for this distinction between inferiorisation and evaluation. Both types of prejudice are forms of inferiorisation, but only hostile sexism is based on the explicit attribution of negative traits.

The second aspect to retain concerns the fact that these forms of inferiorisation (through the attribution of difference) are indirect and hidden expressions of inferiorisation, and are, therefore, not perceived as anti-normative. Consequently, people can express these attitudes without fear of being negatively evaluated in contexts where the anti-prejudice norm is salient. Notwithstanding (or maybe because of this), these expressions indeed organise and justify forms of discrimination, providing a space and an opportunity for the emergence of more radical forms of dehumanisation.

Thirdly, it is important to consider that inferiorisation does not build on the difference in itself, but instead on the meaning that this difference conveys. The difference that merely *distinguishes* is not the difference that inferiorises and the difference that I attribute to myself is not the difference that I attribute to others.

Finally, several theoretical approaches have proposed that the traits used in common sense to distinguish groups and social categories are traits perceived as essences, and therefore as long-lasting, distinctive and exclusive. This commonsense conception about the traits that define groups does not inhibit, however, the malleability of the representation that the majorities construct about themselves or about the minorities. Despite essentialisation, the representation of groups can indeed change and the inferiorisation that took place before is not inevitable today.

On the Roots of the Attribution of Differences
In this paper, we underline the association between the attribution of differences, in the context of relationships between groups, and the processes of identity construction. As we know, lasting and significant group memberships are fundamental factors for personal self-representation in the sense that these contribute to the sense of distinctiveness and to the feeling of personal value. Consequently, it is highly likely that people are motivated to support, promote and defend the value and distinctiveness of the groups to which they belong.

This principle of indissociable connection between personal identity and collective memberships can, by itself, explain the love of one's own group (the country relative to other countries, the religion by comparison to other religions, the culture in reference to other cultures), but does not explain derogation, hostility and the representation of the other as radically different or, in our terms, its ethnicisation.

A large amount of research has invoked the effect of mere cate-gorisation and the principles of assimilation and contrast to explain intergroup antagonism, of which cultural inferiorisation is one manifestation. From Sumner's sociology of the beginning of the twentieth century to the cognitive perspectives emerging in the 1980s, the fascination for a unique explanatory principle has gener-ated an exaggerated attention to the cognitive processes as the roots of intergroup conflict. In the same way, group identification (i.e. the association between the self and any given group) has been proposed as *the* factor stirring intergroup conflict. However, recent analyses of cumulative data from these lines of research have revealed its insufficiencies and the need to look for other variables. We propose that identification only becomes an explanatory factor of intergroup dynamics when another group is represented as threatening our group's identity and the functions that this iden-tity represents: namely, the physical survival of the group and its safety; the value of the group and the positive self-esteem that can be derived from it; the group beliefs about what is true and what is false, about what is positive and what is negative.

Specifically, it is pertinent to underline the importance of the answer that the groups to which we belong give to our need to reduce uncertainty and the possible threat that another group, characterised by other values, can represent to that same need. It is, thus, highly plausible that the attribution of difference and inferiority to another group derives from the need to assure the certainty and coherence of our world view and to protect ourselves from the threat that the mere existence of other world views represents to our system of beliefs.

Aside from the feeling of threat as a moderator of the impact of the degree of group identification on hetero-ethnicisation, some other factors should be stressed. Based on empirical research on close domains, we propose three other moderating factors of the impact of identification on the attribution of difference and inferiority: the normative context, the inclusive or exclusive representation of our own group and the complexity of the system of identifications.

The normative contexts where social relations exist may, in this analytical perspective, be divided into two categories: egalitarian contexts and competitive contexts. Egalitarian contexts are guided by the belief in the equal value that each person is entitled to, regardless of his/her origin or membership, and by the belief in the advantages of cooperation. Competitive contexts are marked by beliefs concerning the advantages of inequality, hierarchy and dominance, beliefs that serve as legitimising myths of inferiorisation. Thus, it is possible to assume that, in egalitarian contexts, the impact of ingroup identification on the representation of the Other as different and inferior is less plausible.

Concerning the second moderating factor of identity effects, some studies show that groups of identification can be theoretically depicted as inclusive or exclusive. In the case of national identity, for example, it is common to distinguish between patriotism (valuing one's own country) and nationalism (an orientation to conflict with other groups), and between a civic and an ethnic conception of nation. It might be expected that national identification associated with nationalistic and ethnic orientations will more easily generate inferiorisation of other nations, peoples or cultures and opens the space for conflict with other groups.

And finally, we propose that an inferiorising representation of the Other, in contexts of cultural, religious or political relations, is more likely in societies or in contexts characterised by the salience of one unique form of categorisation. Social segmentation (or its perception) along one unique dimension and its division in dichotomical terms facilitates conflict and mutual inferiorisation. On the contrary, more complex societies, differentiated along several unrelated social dimensions, may cause the decrease of the association between identification and inferiorisation. Similarly, people with a more complex representation of their identity, through the salience of multiple categorisations, depending less on one single group, may reveal themselves as more tolerant and more able to integrate different cultural perspectives. Indeed multiple social identities facilitate the experience of a diverse and complex world deriving from contact with individuals that are ingroup members in one dimension and outgroup members in another relevant dimension. This variable (complexity of social structure and its psychological correlates) requires, nonetheless, a more thorough analysis. In fact, social contexts nowadays are, to a great extent, characterised by a great complexity but one does not witness an automatic passage between structural complexity and identity complexity. Greater complexity of the world and the frequent crossings of social categories do not necessarily correspond to more cognitive complexity and greater tolerance to incongruence and dissonance.

Can Reified Difference and Similarity be the Source of Antagonistic Relations between Groups?

In the former section, difference was analysed as an 'attributive process', largely dependent on the degree of identification and on the articulation of identification with the feeling of threat, the normative context, the type of representation of the group to which one belongs and the complexity of the system of identifications. That is, difference was conceptualised as the result of psychological and social processes. We now look to differences that are reified, seen as objective, natural and external to individuals' judgements and we ponder on the consequences for the quality of the relationships between groups. That is, difference is now seen as the source of specific patterns of intergroup relations. In this case, however, differences cannot be analysed outside the context of similarities – these too are seen as objective and natural. The question we now posit is to know how we react to a reified difference or similarity and how this reaction articulates with identity.

We start by proposing a hypothesis still insufficiently analysed. To people that are highly identified with their groups, in a context of asymmetrical social relations, a position of dominance may elicit a strong indifference towards difference. The *Other*, once depicted as radically different, is placed outside our world and does not constitute a threat; the Other is put outside the system of comparisons. In some situations, such a group may elicit pity or sympathy; most of the time, however, it will be targeted with indifference. This indifference may go as far as the aestheticisation of the Other's suffering. A few years ago, Susan Sontag published a work on the contemplation of the pain of others, reflecting on the image as the updating of the suffering. But this updating of suffering or its banalisation or denial only occurs with images from 'our world'. At the extreme, suffering in 'another world' may be experienced merely as an aesthetic event.

The problem emerges differently when the Other is not or cannot be placed outside our world. In this case, some reflections and some empirical studies have shown that, to people that are highly identified with the group to which they belong (salient in a given comparative context), threat does not derive as much from difference as it derives from similarity. Indeed, in some circumstances, similarity between social entities seen as distinct may facilitate cooperation and the envisaging of common projects. But it can also happen that similarity is seen as a threat to the group distinctiveness, even as a threat to the group's *raison d'être*. Freud talked about the 'narcissism of small differences', and in social relations we often witness all kinds of strategies that are undertaken to show distance and to expel the ghost of similarity. We witness the horror attributed to similarity in several situations, such as in aesthetic movements, in the field of schools of thought and in religious groups. Conflicts between monotheist religions and the sectarian movements within represent a clear example of this.

Once more, it is the 'burden' of identity that defines this new process that we are now describing. It is the strong identification with the group that turns the Other into a threat to distinctiveness and in this sense the impact of difference and similarity on discrimination will be moderated by the degree of identification with our group. We have experimental evidence to support the hypothesis stating that a minority that abandons its identity to adopt the patterns of the majority (i.e. that nullifies difference) is evaluated more negatively than a minority that remains different. In the context of the relationships between immigrants and a majority, we also have experimental evidence to support the hypothesis that similarity between majority and minority leads to a greater discomfort among those who are highly identified with the majority group. Thus, motivational factors associated with the defence of the group's distinctiveness seem to generate potentially negative intergroup relations from highly identified individuals in a situation of perceived similarity or proximity.

Concerning those that possess low levels of identification with the group to which they belong or situations where this identification is not salient, similarity and cultural proximity can facilitate intergroup relations insofar as it permits those concerned to think in terms of a super-ordinate category of humans, of persons with a common fate. However, among these same persons, when differences between groups become salient, the distance between the groups is augmented and the favouritism benefiting one's own group is exacerbated.

Nevertheless, we advance the hypothesis that difference is also problematic for those who are highly identified with the group when the context is presented as threatening to the group's cultural value. A positive relation with difference requires a secure social identity, in the sense of a feeling of trust and reliability of the group's value, as well as a representation of humans characterised by the value of diversity.

We face a theoretically and empirically complex debate. Hence the need to introduce, in future research, a more thorough articulation between cognitive, motivational, ideological and socio-structural factors. There is enough empirical research to come up with new theorisations, outside the laxity that some post-modernism led us to. We face, however, strong gaps concerning the systematic study of the minorities' points of view, of their projects and reflections. Furthermore, it is important to expand the research to the analysis of relational contexts, confronting majority and minority perspectives (seen as similar and close or seen as different and distant) in order to disentangle the meaning of difference hetero- and self-attributed.

A few years ago, we ended an empirical investigation on the relationship with difference, quoting the novelist and essayist Amin Maalouf in his book *Deadly Identities*. We revisit that quotation. Maalouf talks about how Muhammad-Ali undertook a voluntary 'ocidentalisation' of Egypt, of which he was viceroy at the beginning of the nineteenth century. Muhammad-Ali and Egypt became dangerous to the West, and the European powers sent a joint military offensive against him. Muhammad-Ali was beaten and humiliated. According to Maalouf, 'From this episode the Arabs concluded then and still conclude now that the West doesn't want the rest of the world to be like it; it just wants them to obey it.'

Notes

1 This chapter is based on research that we have been publishing and the literature underlying this work is mentioned there. See especially, J. Vala, C. Pereira and R. Costa-Lopes, 'Is the Attribution of Cultural Differences to Minorities an Expression of Racial Prejudice?' *International Journal of Psychology* 44.1, 2009, pp. 20–28; R. Costa-Lopes, J. Vala, C. Pereira and P. Aguiar, 'A construção social das diferenças nas relações entre grupos sociais' (Social construction of differences within relations between social groups), in M.V. Cabral, K. Wall, S. Aboim and F.C. Silva (eds), *Itinerários: A investigação nos 25 anos do ICS* (Lisbon: Imprensa de Ciências Sociais, 2008), pp. 769–92.

Can We Live Without the Other?

KAREN ARMSTRONG

On the eve of the Suez Crisis, the late Canadian scholar Wilfred Cantwell Smith wrote presciently that unless Muslims managed to come to terms with the modern West, which was now a fact of life, they would fail the test of the twentieth century. But he also added that unless the Christian and the western worlds learned that they shared the planets not with inferiors but with equals, they too would fail the test of the twentieth century. The atrocities of 11 September 2001 showed that neither side had absorbed these lessons satisfactorily. It is ironic that we so constantly hear about a 'clash of civilisations' at a time when our world is bound together – politically, financially and electronically – more closely than ever before. We now know that what happens in Palestine, Iraq and Afghanistan today is likely to have repercussions tomorrow in New York, London or Madrid. In 2001, the new Bush administration had intended to confine its attention to home affairs and in the United Kingdom, the big news story concerned the asylum seekers who, almost daily, tried to enter the country, clinging to the underside of trucks and trains. Britain seemed like a privileged gated community, its ports guarded against the Other by police and sniffer dogs. But on 11 September, it became clear that in our new global village, if you turn your back on the rest of the world, that world is likely to come to you – in a terrible and distorted form.

So we cannot live without the Other. But we are not making a very good job of living with him. There are, of course, many trouble spots in our torn and uneven world, but I am going to confine my brief remarks to the division between the Muslim world and the West. The terrorism that preoccupies us today did not come out of the blue. Cantwell Smith saw problems ahead even before the disreputable Suez Crisis. A long history of missed opportunities on both sides, and short-sided policies, designed to get cheap oil or to secure a strategic position, has alienated a large segment of the Muslim world. The western powers have promoted dictatorial regimes that have helped to radicalise the population: denied normal means of expression, often the only place where people could express their discontent was the mosque. Conflicts that were originally secular have been allowed to fester until they have been sacralised, which makes it all the harder to find a pragmatic solution based on compromise. The obvious example is the Israel–Palestine conflict, which is the symbolic heart of our current problems. It is imperative that we make a concerted effort to find a truly just solution to such conflicts. In an age where increasingly small groups will have the powers of destruction previously the preserve of the nation state, we are unlikely to have a viable world to hand on to the next generation if we do not correct the current imbalance.

I am a religious historian so I am going to concentrate on the religious aspects of our dealings with the Other. In the middle of the twentieth century, it was often assumed that secularism was the coming ideology and that religion would never again play a major role in world affairs. In truth, the source of the current divide is political; what we call – unsatisfactorily in my view – 'fundamentalism' is at base a religiously articulated form of nationalism. It erupted in every major world faith in the latter part of the twentieth century as a rebellion against secular modernity. The vast majority of 'fundamentalists' are not violent; only a tiny proportion takes part in acts of terror. Most are simply trying to live what they regard as a good religious life in a world that seems increasingly hostile to faith. But in regions where violence and warfare have become endemic – the Middle East, Afghanistan, Kashmir – religion has got sucked into the escalating conflict and become part of the problem. Violence affects everything we do: it affects our dreams, fantasies, aspirations, fears and relationships. Not surprisingly, it has affected religion too, compelling those who have become disillusioned with secular policies that never seem to redress their grievances to seek an alternative ideology.

It is important to make this point, because today secularists and religious people seem ranged into two hostile camps. The religious view the secularists as the inimical Other; and secularists see religion itself as the enemy. Just last week in London, militant atheists posted large advertisements on our iconic buses, proclaiming that God is dead. They have said that they feel threatened by the religious imagery that they see on all sides. This is interesting, as Britain must be one of the most secular countries in the world: only 6 per cent of the population attend a religious service regularly. But a large proportion of that 6 per cent are Muslims, who have thus 'bumped up' our national average. Many Britons regard Muslims as Other precisely because they *are* religious. And there is a widespread perception in Europe – dating back to the time of the Crusades – that Islam is an inherently violent faith and an enemy to decent civilisation. I cannot count the number of times I have been informed by members of the general public that Islam is incompatible with democratic modernity.

This is not the case. At the beginning of the twentieth century, every single Muslim intellectual – I can think of only one exception – was in love with the West and wanted their countries to look just like Britain and France. Muhammad Abdu, Grand Mufti of Egypt, hated the British occupation of his country but he felt at home with Europeans and was well-versed in European culture. After a trip to France, he made an intentionally provocative comment. 'In Paris', he said, 'I saw Islam but no Muslims; in Cairo I see Muslims but no Islam.' What he meant was that their modernised economies enabled the Europeans to create a just society that approached the Qur'ānic ideal more closely than was possible in a partially modernised country such as Egypt. In Iran, leading mullahs campaigned alongside secular intellectuals in 1906 for a representational government and constitutional rule. They got their constitution but, two years later, the British discovered oil in Iran and were not going to allow an Iranian parliament to scupper their plans for the oil, which fuelled the British Navy. But immediately after the 1906 Constitutional Revolution, the leading Ayatollah in Najaf proclaimed that the new constitution was the next best thing to the coming of the Shi'ite Messiah, because it would limit the tyranny of the shahs and should, therefore, be supported by every Muslim.

Today nobody can claim the high moral ground. The West has to understand that decades of double standards and inequitable dealings with some Muslim countries have helped to bring us to this unhappy pass. And Muslims have to acknowledge that the recent terrorist atrocities have damaged their cause and that they can no longer be seen as blameless victims. Secularists have to understand that their hostility to religion has helped to bring about the phenomenon of fundamentalism – every single fundamentalist movement that I have studied in Judaism, Christianity and Islam has begun in response to what was perceived as an assault by an invasive, arrogant and sometimes violent secularism. And the religious have to realise that they are, perhaps, not doing enough to promote the irenic, compassionate ideal that lies at the core of every single one of the major traditions. Instead we all of us continue to present ourselves at our most unattractive to the Other.

Let us look briefly at the crisis of the Danish cartoons in 2006. On both sides, it was fuelled by extremists. On one side were the ardent advocates of free speech at all costs, who devised, published and continued to publish the cartoons; on the other, Muslim activists tore down embassies and carried placards, threatening the cartoonists with crucifixion and violent death. The middle ground was ignored. Surveys taken during the crisis revealed that the majority of Danes, while firmly on the side of free speech, were nevertheless distressed that the cartoons had caused such offence. And 97 per cent of the Muslim youth questioned at this time were certainly offended by the cartoons but were horrified by the violent and threatening behaviour of the Muslim activists. But the media ignored this middle ground. As a result, each side presented itself in its worst light, fulfilling the worst expectations of the Other. The 'West' came over as arrogant, contemptuous and insensitive. And the Muslims appeared atavistic, violent and chronically opposed to freedom. When the dust died down, prejudices went a little deeper into the collective psyche.

What we are seeing is a clash not of civilisations but of sanctities. Free speech has become a sacred value in the West; it is inviolable and non-negotiable. But it is essentially a modern value, a luxury that the pre-modern economies – including those of the West – simply could not afford. When people at different stages of the modernisation process share a society, it is inevitable that there will be major differences about our conception of what is sacred. These conflicts are painful because the Other appears to threaten values that are fundamental to our identity. But we simply cannot afford to indulge and even cultivate feelings of righteousness and injury because the stakes are too high. If we are to live together in peace, we have to make a greater effort to understand the point of view of the Other side.

As Cantwell Smith pointed out fifty years ago, western people have to learn that they share the planet with equals – not with inferiors. They have to understand that they have not always been in the vanguard of development. Modernisation is a painful process and it took Europeans and Americans 300 years to develop their secular and liberal institutions. They had the benefit of working according to their own programme and dynamic but even so modernisation was a painful rite of passage that began in the sixteenth century and continued well into the nineteenth. During this time, Europe was wracked by bloody revolutions, reigns of terror, dictatorships, destructive wars of religion and the exploitation of the poor. It is not dissimilar to what is happening in regions that are modernising today.

We must also realise that our 'sacred' values – toleration, free speech, democracy, separation of Church and State – were necessary outgrowths of modernisation. Modernity was not based on a set of ideas but on a fundamental change in the economic basis of society. Instead of relying on a surplus of agricultural produce, like every pre-modern civilisation, modern western society is based on the technological replication of resources and the constant rein-vestment of capital. This freed the western countries from the economic constraints of an agrarian economy. No society before our own could afford the ceaseless changing of the infrastructure that we take for granted. In the pre-modern world, people were not encouraged to have their own ideas and think creatively, because there was little hope of implementing projects that required too much capital outlay. Constantly thwarted originality would lead to frustration and social unrest.

Similarly, democracy was not an idea that was generously dreamed up by western ideologues to give the masses more power. As we know, people had to fight very hard for enfranchisement; the aristocracy did not relinquish power easily. But democracy was found to be essential to modern society. In order to keep the economy expanding, more and more people had to be brought into the productive process, even at a quite humble level, as office workers, printers and factory hands. That meant that they had to acquire a modicum of education. And the more people were educated the more they began to demand a share in the decision-making process of their country. It was discovered – by trial and error – that those countries that democratised forged ahead, while those that tried to confine the benefits of modernity to an elite group fell behind in the march of progress. Democracy is not some-thing that you can apply easily to a country still in the throes of modernisation. It took centuries for the West to develop its demo-cratic institutions.

The same was true of toleration. In order to use all the human resources available to them, groups such as the Jews in Europe and the Catholics in Britain had to be brought into the mainstream. But the shameful atrocities of the 1930s and 1940s showed that this toleration of the Other was only skin-deep. The old mental habits of bigotry and ostracism were still alive and well just beneath the surface. And perhaps they are still there: how else can we account for the recent rise in intolerance and the principled desire to wound or undermine the Other – even in a country like the Netherlands, which until recently had been a beacon of toleration and liberalism in Europe.

People tend to justify a campaign of denigration – the Cartoon Crisis is just one example – by claiming that immigrants must accept the values of the host country that they have chosen to live in. This, of course, is absolutely true and some immigrants are bound to find it a painful and difficult process. But when people say, as they have often said to me, 'This is *my* culture; these people are threatening *our* sacred values', they should perhaps reflect on the colonial project. When the colonial powers imposed their own economy and way of life on a people, they came with force and might (which most immigrants simply do not have) and changed those cultures forever. If we feel inchoately distressed by a threat to our culture, this is nothing compared to the far greater trauma of the colonised people, which lies at the root of many of our current problems.

Countries that were colonised have found it more difficult to modernise. In Europe and America, the two qualities of independence and innovation emerged as the hallmarks of modernity. Without these two characteristics, no matter how many skyscrapers, computers and fighter jets a country may have, it has not acquired the modern spirit. Modernisation in the West was punctuated by declarations of independence on all fronts: religious (Luther declared independence of the Catholic Church); political (the American Declaration of Independence is a classic modernising document); intellectual (scientists and inventors demanded the right to think freely, without the supervision of the religious establishment). And however traumatic modernisation was in the West, it was also exhilarating, because we were always inventing something new, attempting something fresh and finding novel solutions to unprecedented questions.

But in the colonised countries, modernisation did not come with independence but with colonial subjugation. It is interesting to note that Japan, which was never colonised, was able to create its own distinctive and highly successful version of modernity. And instead of being innovative, the colonised peoples were required to imitate us. Modernisation was characterised by dependence and imitation, rather than innovation and independence. The wrong ingredients have gone into the concoction of modernity. If you are making a cake and you do not have fresh eggs but only powdered eggs; if you do not have flour, but only rice; and if you do not have a proper oven, you are not going to get the fluffy cake in the cook book. You might get something very nasty indeed – especially as the cake has to bake far too quickly.

It all comes down to what is called the Golden Rule. Do not treat others as you would not wish to be treated yourself; do not expect from others what you do not ask of yourselves; do not expect Others to respect your pain, perplexity, outrage and fear, if you are not ready to empathise with the pain, perplexity, outrage and fear of the Other. This is surely the basis of civilised society. It is here, I believe, that religion has a real contribution to make to our dilemma. Each of the major world faiths has developed its own version of the Golden Rule and claims that this is the core of religion. No one has expressed this better than Rabbi Hillel, an older contemporary of Jesus. It is said that one day a pagan approached Hillel and promised to convert to Judaism, on condition that Hillel would recite the whole of Jewish teaching while he stood on one leg. Hillel replied: 'That which is hateful to you, do not do to your neighbour. That is the Torah. Everything else is only commentary. Go and learn it!' It is an astonishing statement. There is no mention of God, the creation of the world, the Exodus, Sinai or the Promised Land – all this is simply a 'commentary', a 'gloss' on the Golden Rule.

But this is not what we hear from religious leaders today. Whether they are Jewish, Christian or Muslim, far too many of them seem obsessed with minor issues: orthodox doctrine, sexual ethics, ritual behaviour, or a political option. All these peripheral matters have displaced the central commandment of compassion – the ability to 'feel with' the Other. Compassion, all the traditions say, brings us into the presence of the Sacred, the Divine, God, Nirvana, Brahman, or the Dao, because it forces us to displace ourselves from the centre of our world and put another there, transcending the egotism that holds us back from our best selves. And

yet how very rarely we hear the duty of empathy mentioned today
– at a moment in history where it is more sorely needed than ever.
Instead, because of the behaviour of a few extremists, religion is
associated with hatred, bigotry, intolerance and the denigration of
others.

That is why I am launching a Charter for Compassion on 11
November 2008. People will be able to contribute to the Charter
online, demanding that the religious traditions reassert the
primacy of the Golden Rule; it will be a multilingual, state-of-
the-art website, and you can find it if you Google 'Charter for
Compassion'. Whether we are religious, atheist, agnostic or
secular, all of us who appreciate the importance of the Golden Rule
have a duty to make it a vibrant reality that can challenge the
narrow dogmatism and self-righteous hatred that characterise too
much secular and religious discourse today. It should become cool
to be compassionate; we should also be striving to find practical
ways of implementing the Golden Rule globally, so that we do not
treat other countries or other communities as we would not wish
to be treated ourselves.

Muslims have a head start on the other traditions in one important respect. The Qur'ān is a pluralistic scripture, ideally suited for
our divided world. Every reading of the Qur'ān is prefaced by
invoking the mercy and compassion of God. The bedrock message
of the Qur'ān is not a doctrine but a summons to practical compassion: it is wrong to build up a private fortune; good to share your
wealth fairly; and to create a just and decent society where poor
and vulnerable people are treated with respect. The Qur'ān insists
that every rightly guided religion that teaches this ethic comes
from God; that God has spoken to every people in their own
cultural traditions; that God did not desire the entire world to
belong to a single *ummah*; that each community has its own *din*,
its own sacred way of life; that Muslims must respect the *ahl al-
qitab*, the people of earlier revelations, speaking to them
courteously, saying, 'We believe what you believe; your God and
our God is one and the same'; finally that God formed humans into
tribes and nations 'so that they may get to know one another' –
not to dominate, colonise, exploit, convert, terrorise or denigrate.

This is the voice of Islam that we need to hear today. And people of good will — be they religious or secular — should be ready to hear it and take it to heart. For centuries, Muslims had a far better record of tolerating, appreciating and learning from the Other than western Christians. They can do it again.

The prime challenge and duty of our generation is to build a global community. Any ideology that breeds hatred, contempt and suspicion — be it religious or secular — is failing the test of time. Our western modernity is aggressive. Our technology has enabled us to kill more people with greater efficiency than ever before. Even our discourse is aggressive — in politics, the media, academe; it is not enough for us to seek the truth. We also have to defeat our opponents. It is not surprising that so much religious discourse has absorbed this modern belligerence. We talk a great deal about 'dialogue' today, but it is difficult for us moderns to achieve. Dialogue means that you not only speak but listen — something that we are not very good at in our talkative, opinionated societies. Without a receptive heart that is open to hear the Other — to listen intently to all the underlying fear, pain and rage — dialogue becomes diatribe. It is no use entering a dialogue with the Other unless we are prepared for it to change us, to challenge our preconceptions, and make us look at ourselves and the Other anew. That is the only way that we can hope to 'get to know one another'.

A Quarrel about Diversity?
The Post-Communist Czech Republic
vis-à-vis the New Realities of
Difference

KATERINA BREZINOVA

A pre-World War II era rich in difference in Central Europe gave way to more than four decades of an almost completely homogeneous society in communist Czechoslovakia, where both the realities and the consciousness of ethnic and religious pluralism were suppressed. The democratic changes after 1989, as well as the gradual adhesion of the Czech Republic to the integration process within the European Union, have meant the country is becoming more diverse, its borders more loosened with respect to Iron Curtain times, and its politics more often confronted with the rest of the world.

Though much celebrated in the early 1990s, this has not always been an easy and welcomed process that would conform to expectations, East or West. Almost two decades into the transition, how once again does the increasingly diverse Czech Republic cope with the new realities of difference? What kind of discourse has accompanied the gradual comeback of diversity in the country?

Multiculturalism, the 'Czech Way'?

Over the second half of the twentieth century, the until then heterogeneous region of Central Europe was considerably homogenised in its ethnic composition[1] and, perhaps more importantly, in its imagination. As a former Czech president and playwright Václav Havel once referred to this part of the post-communist heritage, the 'great shroud of uniformity' drove all the remaining 'national and cultural differences into the subterranean areas of social life' and 'created the monstrous illusion that we were all the same'.[2] The memory of those other peoples – namely Jews, Germans, Hungarians – was effectively manipulated by the communist propaganda and/or forgotten. The remaining Other, largely represented by the country's local Roma (Gypsy) population, was perceived as a social 'problem' and dealt with accordingly. The process leading the country from heterogeneity to homogeneity culminated in January 1993 when Czechoslovakia, up to then a federal state of Czechs and Slovaks, split into two independent nation states.

After a decade of marginal existence among scholars and human rights activists, the term 'multiculturalism' came to the forefront of Czech political debate in 2005. Moved by the murder of Theo van Gogh in the Netherlands and later by the terrorist bombings in London, the actual president of the Czech Republic Václav Klaus sparked mainstream interest in the issue from the very top of the political hierarchy by describing multiculturalism as a 'fashionable and leftist evil'[3] and a 'tragic mistake of the contemporary Western civilization' introduced to our country from outside.[4] In his 2008 veto of the Anti-discrimination Act defining the right to equal treatment and banning discrimination passed by the Lower and Upper House of Representatives, Václav Klaus rejected the Bill as 'ideological' and 'dangerous', since in the Czech Republic 'no one is discriminated against'.[5] Others disagree. According to the respected Integration Index findings from 2007, the Czech Republic fares second to worst in the area of protection against discrimination.[6]

The harsh caricatures of multiculturalism cited above are somewhat characteristic of the style of the public debate about social and cultural diversity in the Czech Republic. Above all, the debate has been unclear: words and concepts with multiple interpretations are used at random, so only rarely may one recognise what it is that the speaker in question has in mind when he or she praises or, more often, criticises multiculturalism. Current Czech political discourse about the subject may easily give us the impression that it defends the right of extremists or fundamentalists to pursue their own concepts of the world, amicably or otherwise.

Moreover, Czech critics of multiculturalism tend to blame it for inciting, or even 'deifying', mass immigration and for favouring immigrants at the expense of the local population.[7] While the immigration rate into the Czech Republic has been steadily growing over the last decade, representing now some 2.7 per cent of total population, this number is still shy in comparison with many other countries.[8] The Czech Republic is not (yet) facing the challenges regarding the integration of its foreign-born population and the second generation of immigrants which is true elsewhere, yet local critics of multiculturalism do mirror the backlash against immigration in Western Europe. Subsequently, they feed its arguments into pre-existing Czech isolationist discourse.[9]

Lastly, prevalent critical attacks on multiculturalism in the Czech Republic aim at discrediting this current of thought and its supporters by driving them to the leftist, illiberal, or even extremist side of the playing field. While the idea of multiculturalism was certainly born in the 1960s in liberal and left circles, the term and its politics have since entered the political mainstream in countries across the world and have no intrinsic ideological sign. It was embraced by the conservative government led by Australian Prime Minister John Howard (1996–2007), yet at the same time there exists an important critique of multiculturalism coming from the left.

Which Multiculturalism?

Critical voices against multiculturalism coming from part of the Czech political spectrum represent by no means the only, nor the most important, dispute about the essence and benefits of this model of approaching social and cultural diversity in contemporary societies. Most frequently, informed arguments deal with the multivalent nature of multiculturalism: while some use it to describe the situation in a society where two or more cultures coexist together, others will insist that it is a theory, a way of perception and only later a way of structuring social diversity. Still others are likely to see multiculturalism as a social goal related to specific political programmes. One current of criticism is motivated by multiculturalism's alleged lack of emphasis on linking and mutual influencing of cultures, as well as the danger of forcing individuals into a straitjacket of their − often unfelt − ethnic identity and external, typically outdated folkloristic characteristics presented as a primordial given, and not a choice. Furthermore, other critics warn that political recognition of selected types of otherness steals attention away from other, unrecognised differences. This results in the artificial creation of new social hierarchies that only benefit elites − within the majority or minority − while those truly in need remain marginalised.

These are crucial and relevant questions that must be discussed in connection to ethnic and cultural plurality in contemporary societies, in Europe and worldwide. The term 'multiculturalism' describes different realities in different contexts, indeed. Canada, the USA and Australia, which were among the first countries to formulate multicultural policies, focused them primarily on the rights of indigenous − not immigrant − parts of the population. The term soon passed on to include groups marginalised on other than ethnic grounds, such as gender, religion, sexual identification, or physical or mental disability as well. In Western Europe, the term *multiculturalism* has come to imply immigration from non-European countries.

As an eminent Canadian theorist of liberal multiculturalism Will Kymlicka suggests, the key question is not if we are to accept multiculturalism or not. The real question is which multiculturalism we are to accept. In his view, multiculturalism recognises the cultural and ethnic plurality of contemporary societies and subsequent adoption of policies that will take into account all, albeit somewhat unusual, Czechs or Canadians and support their effective integration in a higher civil framework. Respect to cultural difference neither implies elevating group rights over the individual rights, nor separation of some of the groups. It is, according to Will Kymlicka, rather a consequence of the founding stones of modern liberal-democratic institutions: principles of freedom, justice and equality.[10]

Culture and Power

It seems fitting to wonder at this point why at least a part of the political representation and population in the Czech Republic, as well as in other countries of Central and Eastern Europe, are having trouble with the difference. Is it, in words of a Polish poet, Czeslaw Milosz, due to the other social legacy of communism and cultural heritage of 'the Other Europe'? Is it due to the insufficient contact with the difference?[11] Can it be explained by the weak state, regional or local administrations that mask their lack of efficiency in resolving the practical and often conflicting aspects of everyday multicultural living by culturalisation and ethnicisation of the difference, as some studies on local integration suggest? Is it, as certain Czech politicians propose, because the notions of multiculturalism and intercultural dialogue have been artificially imported to the country from outside – especially due to EU external pressures – and do more harm than good?

The debate about managing culturally, ethnically and linguistically heterogeneous society – regardless whether we choose to name it multiculturalism or intercultural dialogue – will be a delicate topic for a long time to come in the Czech Republic. For what it ultimately represents is a dispute about a new, more open kind of national imagination; a quarrel between an exclusive way of seeing one's own identity and rather inclusive and complementary identities. This kind of imagination, however, is jeopardising the until now dominant purist construct of the 'typical Czech'.[12]

In all probability, the conflict over national imagination would hardly excite Czech politicians if it were taking place on a purely symbolical level. But as is often the case with ethnically defined countries, national identity is very closely linked to institutions of the state, and therefore to power. A number of European countries including the Czech Republic play a hypocritical game when they perceive themselves and their institutions as ethnically neutral. That the contrary is true can be seen by merely glimpsing at textbooks or the programme of the state-funded National Theatre, which have until now successfully ignored national minorities living in the Czech Republic, as well as its immigrant population.

If we are to give a chance to successful and non-conflicting integration of plurality, which de facto exists in the Czech Republic regardless of what some people might think of multiculturalism or intercultural dialogue, it is not enough to ask the Others to consistently respect laws and to assimilate, trying to 'act like other Czechs',[13] or release across-the-board racist accusations of the Czech majority population as often happens. What needs to be modified is the notion of illusory homogeneity of contemporary Czech identity, a legacy of nineteenth-century romantic ideology and, subsequently, the behaviour of government authorities and relevant political institutions on all levels.

A Quarrel about Diversity, or a Quarrel about Modernity?

The events of 2001 in New York and Washington, 2003 in Madrid and 2005 in London led some to revive Samuel Huntington's thesis of the 'clash of civilisations'. Others disagree. Ian Buruma and Avishai Margalit[14] argued that the ideological basis that informs this sometimes dramatic confrontation has less to do with differences between and among different civilisations, but rather with the different attitudes within these civilisations towards modernity as the prevailing historical trend defining the paradigm of the contemporary world.

In this view of history, the clash does not occur between geographical entities (East – West) or 'civilisations' (Islam – Judeo-Christianity), but rather in time and the mind, that is, between the pre- or anti-modern and modern outlooks. Isaiah Berlin observes that the birth of modernity in Europe was not as smooth and unopposed as generally described, and that a formidable intellectual undercurrent had formed in opposition to Enlightenment as the first embodiment of modernity. This counter-Enlightenment cross-current represented first by German romanticism later informed various forms of 'anti-western' ideologies, as well as the competing visions of 'alternative' modernities such as fascism and communism.

The process of Europe's modernisation is important as a point of reference, and especially as a formative element shaping the current European identities. In many narratives of transition in Central and Eastern Europe after 1989, what has been at stake is a process whereby the East should in theory become more like the West. The experience, however, does not always confirm this hypothesis. The post-communist Europe whose national imaginations are still largely heir to German romanticism is witnessing new, emerging forms of modernity, which may or may not really resemble the Western European experience. Important local cross-currents from the backlash against migration and multiculturalism to the re-emergence of ethnic and religious intolerance are being formulated against the new realities of difference in some of the region's countries.

Notes

1 Throughout the second half of the twentieth century, Czechoslovakia established itself as one of the most ethnically homogenous countries in Europe. According to the official Census results from 1970, 65 per cent of the population of Czechoslovakia identified as of 'Czech', 29.3 per cent as 'Slovak', 4 per cent as 'Hungarian' and 0.6 per cent as 'German' nationality. For more than forty years, the only unrestricted contact between the Czechs and other nations was represented by the coexistence with Slovaks within the framework of Czechoslovakia. Czech Statistical Office: www.czso.cz.

2 Václav Havel, 'Understanding Post-Communism'. Excerpt taken from the address by the former Czech president at George Washington University, Washington DC, USA, 22 April 1993.

3 Václav Klaus, *Týden*, 6 December 2004.

4 Václav Klaus, *MfD [Mlada fronta Dnes]*, 16 July 2005.

5 Václav Klaus, Communication from 16 May 2008 to Miloslav Vlček, Head of the Lower House of Representatives. The Czech Republic remains the only European country which has not yet implemented Community regulations. The Anti-discrimination Act should have been adopted before the Czech Republic's accession to the European Union in May 2004. Since then, the European Commission has threatened the Czech Republic several times with a lawsuit at the European Court of Justice for its failure to incorporate EU regulations into national law.

6 MIPEX index produced by the British Council and Migration Policy Group compares all 25 EU member and 3 non-EU countries. Data as of 1 March 2007. Source: www.integrationindex.eu

7 Jiří Payne, advisor to the President Václav Klaus, referred to the 'suicidal steps' of establishing the Schengen free border zone: 'instead of building and guarding the borders, we are opening them to all criminals'. BBC radio interview, July 2005.

8 See Czech Statistical Office data (http://www.czso.cz) and latest Ministry of Labour and Social Affairs data. In 2000, the official statistics registered 200,951 foreigners living in the Czech Republic, out of which some 25 per cent were from Ukraine, 22 per cent from Slovakia, 12 per cent from Vietnam, 8 per cent from Poland and 6 per cent from Russia. Those numbers almost doubled by 2007 when 392,315 foreigners lived in the country.

9 According to an international sociological survey carried out in 1995, the attitudes to foreigners and to immigration tended to be rather isolationist and could be best described by the words 'fear', 'mistrust' or 'caution'. Ninety per cent of respondents in 1995 supported the affirmation that the Czech Republic should take stronger measures against illegal immigrants. See Alena Nedomová and Tomáš Kostelecký, 'The Czech National Identity', *Czech Sociological Review* 5.1, 1997. In 2007, 75 per cent of Czech respondents called for further restriction and control of the immigration. Moreover, they tended to link their concerns about immigration with worries about identity: 74 per cent supported the statement that 'our way of life must be protected'. See Pew Research's *47-Nation Pew Global Attitudes Survey*, October 2007.

10 Will Kymlicka, *Multicultural Citizenship: A Liberal Theory of Minority Rights* (Oxford: Oxford University Press, 1995).

11 2007 Eurobarometer Survey concerning Intercultural Dialogue in Europe concluded that 'the more intercultural contacts people have,

the more they are likely to perceive them as beneficiary'. See Gallup Organisation Flash EB No 217, Intercultural Dialogue in Europe, 2007.
12 Sociological findings indicated that a 'typical member of the Czech society' would be best described as a Czech-speaking person of Czech citizenship and Czech origin, who lives in the same town or village or at least close to his/her birthplace: 98.9 per cent of respondents said they spoke only Czech at home; 99.7 per cent of them held Czech citizenship and 90.2 per cent declared themselves as being of Czech ethnic heritage. No wonder the respondents did not see any point in distinguishing between Czech state citizenship and nationality: being 'truly' Czech means automatically having both. See International Sociological Survey Program conducted in 1995, details in Nedomová and Kostelecký, 'The Czech National Identity'.
13 Václav Klaus, *MfD [Mlada fronta Dnes]*, 16 July 2005.
14 Ian Buruma and Avishai Margalit, *Occidentalism: The West in the Eyes of Its Enemies* (New York: Penguin, 2004).

Vulnerability, Spaces and the Building of Borders

MANUELA RIBEIRO SANCHES

Distance and Proximity, Universality and Particularity

… one evening when we were sitting out in the garden she [my
grandmother] wanted to know whether she would be able to
see the border between India and East Pakistan from the plane.
When my father laughed and said, why, did she really think the
border was a long black line with green on one side and scarlet
on the other, like it was on a school atlas, she was not so much
offended as puzzled.

No, that wasn't what I meant, she said. Of course not. But
surely there's something – trenches perhaps, or soldiers, or guns
pointing at each other, or even just barren strips of land. Don't
they call it no man's land?[1]

This excerpt, taken from *The Shadow Lines* by Amitav Ghosh, tells
us, among other things, of empires and the new nations that sprang
from them. These empires created contacts and vulnerabilities,
borders characterised by the tension between proximity and
distance. It is these frontiers that, albeit in other contexts, still feed

many of the reflections about what we now tend to call intercultural dialogue.

However, for reasons that I hope to make clear later on, rather than this term I prefer to use the expression 'contact zone'. Mary Louise Pratt proposed this concept to describe phenomena of cultural interchange,[2] in which reciprocal influences, the unstable frontiers (more or less imposed), are developed according to processes that have less to do with interculturality and more to do with transculturation, a concept that the author borrowed from the Cuban anthropologist Fernando Ortiz to describe the complex processes of reciprocal and unequal influence that characterised American society during the 'conquest'.

To speak of contact zones amounts to speaking of distance and proximity, but, above all, of the precarious and political nature of cultural borders and their inequalities. The way in which these concepts are articulated determines the way in which we define and question theories and practices of intercultural dialogue, questions of multiculturalism and citizenship.

I shall depart tentatively, heuristically, from two general premises that depend on the adopted perspective: distance encourages the use of universals, leading to the blurring and questioning of frontiers, whereas proximity promotes particularity and the need to draw boundaries, thereby accentuating differences.[3]

The question of universality and particularity has also played a decisive role with regard to the way in which the interdependencies and relationships formed in the age of globalisation have been theorised and analysed, as well as practised and experienced.

Some approaches have underlined the fact that globalisation does not result only in the homogenisation of a world that has shown itself to be persistently made up of heterogeneities.[4] In fact, these can be reinforced through complex and contradictory processes that, endowed with a more or less diffuse and deterritorialised structure (one that is more cellular and less vertebral), make it possible for there to be new configurations of violence.[5] These trends would explain the need for an intercultural dialogue, hesitating between, on the one hand, proximity – guaranteed by the ever more rapid exchanges of goods and ideas in (cyber)space, or the increasing mobility of people – and, on the other hand, the distance generated, for example, by the so-called 'clashes' – real or virtual – of 'civilisations'.[6]

On the other hand, both global flows and the interactions arising from them have been countered by the distance created by material borders, such as those of Fortress Europe, legitimising the fences erected in Melilla, the patrolling of the Mediterranean and Atlantic coastal areas in order to stem the incoming tides of beings who, deprived of any citizenship rights, are considered subhuman,[7] beings who, dead or alive, find themselves reduced to the level of mere statistics in the anxious accounting of an *apartheid* Europe,[8] persistently hanging on to a collective national imagination based on purity,[9] despite the transnationality of the European Union.

However, while it is true that globalisation and the migratory flows arising therefrom have been questioning the clear separation between the First and the Third World,[10] the fact remains that new territorialisations have been taking place, namely through the creation of private condominiums or shopping centres that transfer the public urban space to private and strictly demarcated territories, as a way of guaranteeing security; especially when faced with the so-called 'immigrants' or 'ethnic minorities' – who, in their turn, are territorialised in 'problem neighbourhoods', despite all the rhetoric of 'integration', multiculturalism or interculturality.

The 'fear of small numbers', based upon what Appadurai calls 'predatory narcissisms',[11] themselves derived from a conception of the nation as being founded on soil and blood,[12] may therefore be understood as a necessary moment in the building of a border separating those who belong from those who are only partly welcome, or, in other words, the 'Others'.

One is therefore faced with an example that is less of a dialectic than a conflict of particular, asymmetric, interests, which therefore proclaim the need for the 'Other' to be 'tolerated'. However, the respective definition is not questioned, therefore the 'Self' is posited not as an effective interlocutor but as an authority that determines the so-called 'universal' principles on which these 'encounters' with 'difference', in other words 'intercultural dialogue', should be based.

Besides the distinctions and limits, or, in other words, the frontiers that are generated by global flows, one also has to consider discourses on *métissage*, *Creolisation* and hybridity that circulate with increasing visibility, even in the media, in order to foster proximity in an ever more global, but more divided world, whether in the name of the 'war on terror' or in the name of 'western decadence'. At the same time, we are witnessing the commoditisation of difference, which always seems to sell very well. The exotic makes what is near seem distant, tolerable, when reduced to a mere multicultural ornament; on the other hand, the great transnational enterprises know full well to what extent globalisation has not only fostered effective cosmopolitanism and democratised it, but also reinforced the most limited forms of parochialism, together with legitimate demands centred upon the local.

Consequently, it can be said that proximity and distance, local and global, particular and universal, are concepts that may be thought of and practised in a multiform and complex fashion. On the one hand, they are used with objectives and programmes that are quite distinct from one another, not to say actually antagonistic. See, for example, the way in which the argument of the defence of western civilisation is used to postulate a universal humanism and the defence of human rights (with special emphasis being given to those of women), in order to promote imperial interests or interventions; or, as a counterpart to this, the way in which these same rights are invoked by the 'Others' to promote alternative forms of female emancipation or ways of preserving difference, or, in other words, culture. This is the case with some minorities in Europe or indigenous groups, especially in non-European areas.

Hence, distance and proximity cannot be equated in a simplistic manner to universality and particularity; given the complex way in which borders are drawn and negotiated, difference is produced – imposed or claimed – in different ways, with greater or lesser degrees of antagonism and convergence.

Is there another way of analysing proximity and distance in relation to the question of cultural difference? How are universals to be articulated with the virulence of the differentialist antagonisms to be found at a global level, or with other forms of vulnerability caused by close encounters with difference? I believe that a possible answer to this question may be found in the way in which this difference is produced,[13] borders between cultures are drawn and constructed.

The complexity of these themes, it may also be said, takes on different nuances, depending on the viewpoint that one adopts in order to consider them. As we draw nearer or move further away, alter our focal point, the observed objects display different degrees of complexity.

In order to respond more precisely to these themes that so far I have merely sketched out, I propose adopting a series of different angles or viewpoints, ranging from the most distant to the nearest, using spatial categories that I shall articulate with temporal ones, that is, adopting a historical perspective, remaining fully aware of the relative nature of these two Kantian a priori. These show themselves to be social constructions, which help to explain the way in which questions of proximity and distance are framed, the way in which we draw borders and boundaries, and thus determine who has 'culture' and who is 'different'.

The path that I propose to follow is based less on concepts than on images. In a world that is marked by the ubiquity of what has come to be called visual culture, I propose a reading that is based less on the idea that we are manipulated by the power of the visual, and more on the Benjaminian hypothesis of thinking through images, in the literal sense. To illustrate my argument I shall consider a wide range of images, namely a series of maps, almost all of which are examples of what Woodward and Lewis call mental maps:

> The map is at the juncture of performance and artifact, of the visual and the aural, of the static and the dynamic. It sheds light on such deeply ingrained and universal human needs as wayfinding and feeling 'in place'. Maps have acted as versatile and essential tools for visual thinking about the world at global, continental, national, and local scales. They have shaped scientific hypotheses, formed political and military strategies,

formulated social policy, and reflected cultural ideas about the landscape, and they have been agents of social and political power. They have also communicated, explained, and preserved information essential to the survival of cultures.[14]

A Question of Scale

Viewed from afar, the globe seems to suggest a shared place, a point of anchorage in an unknown universe. Differences tend to dissipate in favour of a common destiny, with similar aims and dangers. Universals appear as a concrete possibility, less a generalising abstraction or imposed homogenisation – globalisation – than a common task for a planet under threat.

The continents appear to be secondary when compared with the oceans, which seem less to surround them, and to separate them, than to make them possible. The frontiers between nations are not visible, as we imagine from political maps that we frequently identify with 'cultures',[15] for example those of a 'Europe of diversity'. We do not even manage to make out the 'tribal' borders of the ethnographic maps, marking out the boundaries of the peoples that we still insist on situating on the edge of Europe, in some of the more recondite areas of Asia, and, above all, in Africa.

Like the father of the protagonist of *The Shadow Lines* by Amitav Ghosh – explaining to the grandmother, the day before she went to visit her relatives in the recently created Pakistan, that, when she flew over the Indian subcontinent, she wouldn't recognise the boundaries that the skirmishes in the streets close to her house had created and, with them, the vulnerability of human existence – we don't manage to see distinct frontiers, not even those that are dictated by nature itself. Viewed from afar, our planet does not allow a fixed point of view or a single perspective that may provide us with a grounding for positing ethnocentric universals, which reveal themselves to be mere hypotheses, vain or megalomaniac designs.

To put it another way: seen from afar, the conceptions of a panoptic power are denied, the scale pointing to the futility of any attempt to control the whole planet. Viewed from afar, the globe instead shows the ephemeral and constructed nature of borders and boundaries, their entirely historical nature, and their dependence on ideas of space and power that cease to be understood as definitive and much less as universal. The vulnerability of frontiers, of humans and their planet, contrary to what Hegel had maintained from his perspective – only apparently universal, but geographically situated[16] – becomes evident, with everybody, humans and non-humans alike, sharing the risks of an unsustainable development.[17] But the recognition of this vulnerability cannot found a universal law that takes into account the particular encounters between individuals and cultures, in a physical or virtual proximity that, by allowing us to recognise difference, may also create distinctions, borders and barriers and other forms of vulnerability arising from more or less asymmetric or violent interchanges.

In what follows I suggest a series of enlargements, successively drawing closer, in order to map ways of postulating, constructing, difference and the frontiers that produce it. I shall also consider the vulnerabilities that a local proximity can arouse, while articulating them with more global perspectives.

Enlargements and Approaches: Cartography, Power and
Imagined Borders
It is known how cartography changed with the advent of the modern era in the West, namely the way in which the methods based on empirical experience made it possible to find a new way of mapping the planet. Ptolemaic cartography was substituted by Portulan Charts and more precise maps that added a detailed drawing of coasts and continents, based on the experience of navigation, to the symbolic and narrative structure of earlier representations.[18]

Such an alteration was traditionally considered by western historiography as a sign of progress, as an affirmation of objective science and knowledge, according to the prevalent belief in mimetic transparency that was to find an echo in the precise and subjective perspective of Renaissance painting.

This cartographic attention to detail was interpreted as arising from the era of the discoveries that had begun with the so-called 'Portuguese overseas expansion'. These discoveries would, in fact, have been impossible without the help of the Genoese and Catalan school which had, as is known, also benefited in turn from Arab knowledge.[19] Each bay, each inlet therefore begins to correspond to a land that has been discovered and is to be controlled, whether through trade or through its effective future occupation. Maps now make it possible for us to recognise features more clearly, with continents standing out from the ocean, which is now seen as separating and connecting territories,[20] and which political cartography will fill with frontiers between tribes, peoples and nations.

But this was only one possible way of representing the surface of the Earth and its human marks, as can be deduced from a comparison of two maps of Tenochtitlan made by the 'discovered' and the 'discoverers', in which the narrative and symbolic elements of México culture clash with the Euclidian perspective of the conquistadors.[21]

One might also think of the planisphere of Al-Idrisi,[22] in which the south is represented at the top, giving us a sense of vertigo, the feeling of a world upside down, which we have now grown accustomed to in the times of Google Earth, a familiarity that was, however, unthinkable in the period when these 'new worlds' were beginning to be conquered.

One could also remember the history of the discovery of the antipodes of Europe in the age of the Enlightenment. According to the specialists, the precision achieved in mapping was to reach a decisive point with James Cook, who recurring to the two coordinates – something which was only made possible through the invention of the chronometer – was able to draw detailed maps of the islands situated in the immense Pacific Ocean.[23] The great discovery of his second circumnavigation (1772−75) was the non-existence of terra firma in the Antarctic, as had previously been imagined, according to the laws of symmetry, a negative discovery to be added to another equally negative result, namely, the fact that no member of the crew had died of scurvy, thanks to the prophylactic health measures that had been introduced, in which a diet rich in vitamin C had proved to be decisive.

This prosaic heroism echoes in the precision of the map of Tahiti,[24] a place that was, however, to gain a mythical status in the western collective imagination, as the place of a rediscovered paradise,[25] a new upside-down world, a new model for imagining an alternative to a Europe that had reached the peak of its expansion and conquest, with all that now remained being simply to fight for the hegemony over the planet, especially its oceans.

In fact, scientific objectivity did not exclude, rather reinforced, subjective representations, as well as the association of both aspects with the colonial enterprise: nature and exotic fauna and flora were subjected to a universal taxonomy[26] in which humans, the 'Others', were also included, tolerated, as long as they were submitted to the principle of a cultural and racial hierarchical order.[27]

But subjective representations were also linked to the leisure moments of those who stayed at home, but consumed the products that were brought to them as a result of distant travel – tea, sugar, cocoa and coffee – providing them with a source of sociability and Enlightenment in the public space,[28] where they could discuss the ideals of citizenship and future bourgeois revolutions. George Steiner identifies café culture as specifically European, forgetting to mention the trafficking, including that of humans, which made it possible for these products, spices and drugs, to arrive at the tables of colonial Europe's cosmopolitan centres.[29]

But opting for this alternative point of view means making use of other cartographies, mapping out persistent exchanges, prior to the 'era of Portuguese expansion', between Europeans and the peoples without history,[30] until the emergence of the modern world-systems, in which slavery was to prove a decisive moment.[31]

To which one could also add other cartographies from the Pacific, such as the stick charts of Polynesia, which point to other histories and discoveries that, when seen from an excessively localised or distanced viewpoint – excessively particular and only supposedly universal – it is impossible to make out.

These images – more or less enlarged – point to various different, but complementary, ways of representing a world that was intended to be divided into 'West' and 'East', 'North' and 'South', 'tradition' and 'modernity'. A modernity that would be the place of abstraction and universal history, in short of 'civilisation', of the 'West', with its 'Others' being limited to the world of particular cultures, closed in upon themselves, with tribes, ethnic groups and places that are devoid of history. In short, places that are 'different'.

Seen from Close Up: The Nation and
(Post-)Colonial Histories

Maps consequently tell us a great deal about viewpoints of varying distances, as well as about the way in which the positioning of one's perspective exerts power and constructs difference. But they tell us very little about the concrete circumstances under which that power is either exercised or challenged, namely, on an everyday basis in concrete places,[32] despite all the emphasis that is currently placed on deterritorialisation.

Hence the importance of paying attention to the way in which difference – that is, culture – has been produced in contexts of unequal power,[33] thereby contributing to xenophobic differentialisms and a reified concept of irreducible difference, be it racial or cultural,[34] a concept recently bandied about by the defenders of Fortress Europe, and especially of the European nations, understood less as the result of the building of historically determined borders and boundaries than as pure and unchangeable realities, a model that frequently ends up contaminating those that have been excluded from it.[35]

These considerations lead me to situate myself now at a more localised viewpoint as far as the framework of my analysis is concerned. And I shall also evoke yet another two maps.

The first is the famous Pink Map, which appeared in the context of the Berlin Conference (1884).[36] This was to be followed by the English Ultimatum (1890), the high point in terms of exacerbated imperialism and nationalism, in Europe, in general, and in Portugal, in particular. The 'Portuguese nation' finally discovered its imperial vocation and projected it retrospectively, invoking the right to its African territories, for reasons of 'historical presence', that is, a common law, based on difference, a difference that was gradually defined as racial difference, in order, just like other imperial powers, to justify a 'civilising mission' in Africa, an empire on which the nation's integrity also depended.[37] The maps of the African colonies, drawn with great precision and with the marking of the routes of the Portuguese expeditions across the 'heart of darkness', show how its 'civilising mission' was, above all, a fight between European nations and powers.

This interdependence between nation and empire is also clearly expressed in the map with the title 'Portugal is not a small country', part of the propaganda produced at the height of the *Estado Novo* (New State), at the 1934 Colonial Exhibition held in Porto.[38]

Although I am interested in historical considerations, I also find the way in which we *now* interpret this imperial cartography to be particularly pertinent. Compared with the images that I began by presenting, this map traces clear frontiers, superimposing nations and colonies, and thus pointing unwittingly towards the close relationship between European nations and their empires, as well as showing how Europe, as a whole, also fell prey to a shared history of rivalries, disputes and colonial wars.

In fact, the history of Europe could be told from a point of view that brings together and compares the various contributions made by the different nations, in their relations with their imperial projects.[39] Such a perspective might give us less the impression of common realisations produced in the name of progress and a superior civilisation, and enable us instead to recognise the way in which western modernity is closely bound up with other darker moments, a theme that was already outlined by Walter Benjamin in his writings about the philosophy of History.[40] Grounded in a critique of historicism, that form of knowledge which is based on positive facts and objectivity, and which, in the end, shows itself to be a narrative that silences the defeated, Benjamin proposes instead a temporal perspective that interrupts the homogenous time of History, this being a conception that, as Benedict Anderson demonstrated, was, in fact, central to the emergence of the modern European nations as imagined communities.[41]

Theodor W. Adorno and Max Horkheimer[42] also denounced the similarities that they could detect between Nazi modernity and North American economic liberalism, affinities that they also traced back to a founding time of the West, to its 'cultural roots', using Ulysses and his astuteness as an example of a Machiavellian form of Enlightenment that used means to achieve ends, ends that, in themselves, could not be classified as rational. A question that, in the postwar period, was returned to once more by Aimé Césaire in his *Discourse on Colonialism*, challenging Europe to rethink itself and to reflect upon the way in which the Holocaust was only denounced because it related to Europeans.[43] Racism, inherited from colonialism, was therefore to be the great challenge faced by a Europe rebuilding itself from the rubble of World War II.

In fact – and once again presenting a closer perspective – the histories (in the plural) of the 'Portuguese empire' enable us to see a very different image, when compared with the still predominant, and not always explicit, narrative of an exemplary colonialism, in its tolerance and capacity for interacting with the 'Other'.

From the 'Portuguese presence' in the Far East[44] to the notion of a civilising mission – beginning in the late nineteenth century, with the first signs of interest in the colonisation and later the pacification of the African territories – the discourse legitimising the Portuguese colonisation was based, just as happened with other European nations, on the idea of the 'natural inferiority' of the subjugated peoples. On the other hand, the whole of History – and not the histories – of the 'Portuguese colonial empire' could be narrated on the basis of the Middle Passage and slavery.

But let me zoom in again to present an even closer perspective. The African presence in Portugal, studied, for example, by José Ramos Tinhorão and Didier Lahon, is a constant feature in the toponymy of the city of Lisbon.[45] More than these traces, however, I am interested in highlighting the way in which such interchanges in these contact zones can be interpreted less as examples of tolerance and miscegenation than as the result, above all, of the 'Portuguese presence' in Africa.

In this way, it is not surprising that, over the centuries, the representations of black people in Portugal have been – and still are today – representations of subordinate people, jovial to a greater or lesser extent, aggressive to a greater or lesser extent, but almost always 'primitive'. Consider the references that tend to be reproduced in a vicious circle, relating to their participation in everyday life, particularly in the city of Lisbon, in musical sessions and other festivities. Is there a substantial difference between these representations and those of Lisbon as a hybrid or Black city, where 'Lusophonia' music – ranging from Cape Verdian rap to the *kuduro* circulating between Lisbon and Luanda – is marketed as an emblem of the capital's cosmopolitanism, while the questions of an effective citizenship is hardly addressed?

Significantly, the auto-stereotypes regarding the exceptionalism of Portuguese hybridity[46] or its 'gentle customs' are increasingly contradicted by the discourses of both the media and politicians. And these do no more than reproduce and feed national consensuses about the association – by no means exclusive to Portugal – between immigration and crime. But it is never very clearly specified to what extent such difference tends to be an important element for structuring the way in which, through our representations, by constructing the 'Other', we represent 'ourselves', creating strict borders between those who belong entirely and those who will find it hard to enjoy this right.

This, once again, amounts to questioning the notion of the difference to be found in the idea of 'intercultural dialogue'. How are proximity and distance constructed? How are borders produced?

Cartography, Syncopation: Other Spaces, Other Times beyond the Nation

I insist on the closest viewpoint, the one that is nearest to the ground and which takes us away from maps and their epistemological and aesthetic challenges, in order to consider the challenges that our everyday encounters make possible, catalyse and stimulate, recognising how they determine the way in which we tend to draw borders and therefore 'cultures'. The idea of culture as difference is, above all, questionable when the power relations through which the 'Other' is constructed are ignored. After all, who, in the end, has culture?[47] The 'different' person, who in this way is constructed as someone distant, irretrievably distant, despite the fact that, or precisely because, he is so close? Exoticism functions well at a distance. When the 'Other' comes too close, borders and boundaries have to be created in order to contain the difference of the stranger who has come to stay.[48]

Recognising the Black presence in Portugal – to return to the example that I used – may amount to a mere exoticising form of paternalism, in which 'culture' and 'difference' do not find other forms of representativeness beyond those granted through well-intentioned, but no less racist, intercultural policies that substitute, through equivocal practices of representation, those who, in the end, are left without a voice. Besides the territorialised differences – in Martim Moniz, Cova da Moura, Quinta da Fonte – attention should be paid to those contact zones in which 'natives' of different 'origins' intermingle and interact, negotiating borders and vulnerabilities, in a tense balance between distance and proximity. This should not, of course, lead one to ignore various forms of racism, particularly the institutional one.

Opting for this perspective implies choosing an interpretation that is based more on time than on space, an everyday present that cannot ignore the way in which we read the past that made it possible and which also determines the way in which we imagine the future both within and beyond the nation; or, in other words, what we want to be is also defined by the way in which, in the present, we interpret what we were. Which requires less the rewriting of history and more its questioning, paying attention to the silences and the (im)possibility of recovering them.[49] A cartography of the past and the present should consist less of the capacity to give the 'Other' a voice than learning to listen[50]: languages, music, images, heteroglossias, made up from encounters and divergences, conflicts, in contact zones.

In short, it is a question of emphasising the practices of everyday conviviality[51] which are not limited to the exoticism of a post-modern and postcolonial, more or less 'hybrid', Lisbon, but where the proximity and distance created by (neo-)colonial histories are permanently negotiated, where borders are redrawn. In their proximity and distance. With their vulnerabilities.

What other worlds less Portuguese-speaking and more multi-lingual – effectively hybrid or Creolised[52] – will be possible in a Europe that is increasingly being built as a fortress? What heterogeneity of histories will help to provincialise Europe[53] and to deprovincialise Portugal, a nation still overly attached to discourses of national and ethnic difference in relation to majorities and minorities and which therefore betrays the fear of contamination and an ambivalent relationship with the colonial past? How can we explain our having joined in a 'European' or 'western' overmodernity (Augé) – paradoxically the site of the unpolluted and of a supposed hybridity that is frequently limited to tolerating the Other or to proclaiming 'the year of intercultural dialogue' – and the persistence of monolithic historical discourses or imperial cartographies?

These questions might be summarised as follows, returning once more to my starting point and reformulating the question: when will we begin to effectively practise universals that are less imposed than negotiated, both within and beyond the nation? When will there be a 'tactical humanism', aware of the similarities and differences, recognising that we are more than simple robots programmed by 'cultural patterns', and, hence, distinct humans that nonetheless may share the same vulnerabilities?[54] When will there be one 'whole world', a 'common place', a world that is more multilingual,[55] more willing to listen to the counterpoint[56] (note my increasing emphasis on analogies with time and music), to the syncopation of more plural histories?[57]

Questions that I prefer to the certainties of a universal history, like a single book, a monochord, devoid of doubts or futures, preferring to opt for attention to particularities, beyond and within the nation, and the way in which they are imposed or claimed by those who, sometimes, have little more than their own 'culture'.

Above all, what interests me is a more vulnerable way of thinking about identity and difference, universality and particularity, based less on nations or continents and more upon the seas that have long been sailed and thus belong to everybody and nobody at the same time.

As Edouard Glissant reminds us:

The archipelic mode of thought suits the pace of our worlds. It borrows from them its ambiguity, fragility, its derivative drift. It yields to the practice of rerouting, which is neither flight nor renunciation. It acknowledges the scope of the imaginary constructions of the Trace, which it ratifies. Does this mean to abrogate self-control? No, it means, precisely, to be in harmony with whatever in the world is scattered through archipelagoes, these kinds of diversity of extent that join shores and horizons together. We become aware of what was continental, thick and weighing heavy on us, in lavish reflection on that system which until our own times has governed the History of humanity and which is no longer appropriate to the explosiveness of what we experience, neither to our histories nor to our no less lavish acts of errantry. Thinking of the archipelago, of archipelagos, opens these oceans to us.[58]

Acknowledgements

Carlos Branco Mendes, Fernando Clara, Leonor Pires Martins, Ella Shohat and Robert Stam.

Notes

1 Amitav Ghosh, *The Shadow Lines* (Boston, NY: Mariner, 2005 [1988]), p. 148.
2 Mary Louise Pratt, *Imperial Eyes: Travel Writing and Transculturation* (London and New York: Routledge, 1992).
3 Fredrik Barth, *Ethnic Groups and Boundaries* (Bergen: Universitets-forlaget; London: Allen & Unwin, 1969).
4 Arjun Appadurai, *Modernity at Large: Cultural Dimensions of Globalization* (Minneapolis, MN: University of Minnesota Press, 1996); John Tomlinson, *Globalization and Culture* (Chicago: University of Chicago Press, 1999); Stuart Hall, 'Old and New Identities, Old and New Ethnicities', in Anthony D. King (ed.), *Culture, Globalization, and the World-System: Contemporary Conditions for the Representation of Identity* (Minneapolis, MN: University of Minnesota Press, 1997), pp. 45–68; idem, 'Culture, Community, Nation', in David Boswell and Jessica Evans (eds), *Representing the Nation: A Reader. Histories,*

Heritages, Museums (London and New York: Routledge, 1999), pp. 33–44; Anna Lowenhaupt Tsing, *Friction: An Ethnography of Global Connection* (Princeton, NJ and Oxford: Princeton University Press, 2005).

5 Arjun Appadurai, *Fear of Small Numbers: An Essay on the Geography of Anger* (Durham, NC: Duke University Press, 2006), pp. 21, 31–35.

6 In this regard, and for an alternative reading to that of Huntington, see Edward W. Said, 'The Clash of Definitions: On Samuel Huntington', in *Reflections on Exile and Other Essays* (Cambridge, MA: Harvard University Press, 2000), pp. 569–90.

7 Paul Gilroy, *After Empire: Melancholia or Convivial Culture* (London and New York: Routledge, 2004); idem, 'Foreword: Migrancy Culture and a New Map of Europe', in Heike Raphael Hernandez (ed.), *Blackening Europe: The African American Presence* (New York and London: Routledge, 2004); Etienne Balibar, *We the People of Europe: Reflections on Transnational Citizenship* (trans. James Swendon; Princeton, NJ: Princeton University Press, 2005); Iain Chambers, *Mediterranean Crossings: The Politics of an Interrupted Modernity* (Durham, NC: Duke University Press, 2008).

8 Balibar, *We the People of Europe*.

9 Paul Gilroy, *The Black Atlantic: Modernity and Double Consciousness* (Cambridge, MA: Harvard University Press, 1993); Verena Stolcke, 'New Boundaries, New Rhetorics of Exclusion in Europe', *Current Anthropology* 36.1, 1995, pp. 1–24; Appadurai, *Modernity at Large*.

10 See, for example, Tomlinson, *Globalization and Culture*.

11 Appadurai, *Fear of Small Numbers*.

12 Stolcke, 'New Boundaries'.

13 Akhil Gupta and James Ferguson, 'Beyond Culture: Space, Identity and the Politics of Difference', *Cultural Anthropology* 7.1, 1992, pp. 6–23.

14 David Woodward and Malcolm G. Lewis, 'Introduction', in Woodward and Lewis (eds), *The History of Cartography*. Vol. 2, Book 3: *Cartography in the Traditional African, American, Arctic, Australian, and Pacific Societies*, University of Chicago Press, 1998). www.press.uchicago.edu/Misc/Chicago/907287.html

15 Gupta and Ferguson, 'Beyond Culture'.

16 For an interpretation of Hegel's philosophy, from a postcolonial perspective, see Ranajit Guha, *History at the Limit of World-History: Italian Academy Lectures* (New York: Columbia University Press, 2002).

17 Anna Lowenhaupt Tsing, 'The Global Situation', *Cultural Anthropology* 15.3, 2000, pp. 327–60 (331ff.).

112   *Can There Be Life Without the Other?*

18 Maria Fernanda Alegria, João Carlos Garcia and Francesc Relañ, 'Cartografia e Viagens', in Francisco Bethencourt and Kirti Chaudhuri (eds), *História da expansão portuguesa*. Vol. 1. *A formação do Império (1415–1570)* (Lisbon: Círculo dos Leitores, 1998), pp. 26–61.

19 José Mattoso, 'Antecedentes medievais da expansão portuguesa', in Francisco Bethencourt and Kirti Chaudhuri (eds), *História da expansão portuguesa*. Vol. 1. *A formação do Império (1415–1570)* (Lisbon: Círculo dos Leitores, 1998), pp. 12–25; Alegria et al., 'Cartografia e Viagens'.

20 Georg Wilhelm Friedrich Hegel, *Vorlesungen über die Philosophie der Geschichte*, in Eva Moldenhauer and Karl Markus Michel (eds), *Werke*, vol. 12 (Frankfurt am Main: Suhrkamp, 1991), pp. 105–146.

21 See the analysis of these maps in Doreen Massey, *For Space* (London, Thousand Oaks, CA; New Delhi: Sage, 2005), on which I base my argument here.

22 Available online at http://classes.bnf.fr/idrisi/grand/9_05.htm.

23 See, for instance, the chart available at the National Maritime Museum site at http://www.nmm.ac.uk/collections/displayRepro.cfm?reproID =F0295&picture=1#content. On Cook's second voyage around the world see George Forster, *A Voyage around the World* (ed. Nicholas Thomas and Oliver Bernhof; Honolulu: University of Hawaii Press, 2000).

24 See online at http://www.nzetc.org/tm/scholarly/tei-BeaCapt.html.

25 As, for example, in William Hodges's painting, *Vaitepiha Bay, Tahiti*, held at the London Maritime Museum.

26 Tsing, 'The Global Situation'.

27 Manuela Ribeiro Sanches (ed.) (in collaboration with Adriana Veríssimo Serrrão), *A invenção do 'Homem'. Raça, Cultura e História na Alemanha do século XVIII* (Lisbon: Centro de Filosofia da Universidade de Lisboa, 2002).

28 Jürgen Habermas, *Strukturwandel der Öffentlichkeit: Untersuchungen zu einer Kategorie der bürgerlichen Gesellschaft* (Darmstadt und Neuwied: Luchterhand, 1963).

29 George Steiner, *The Idea of Europe* (Tilburg: Nexus Institute, 2004). See also Hall, 'Old and New Identities'; and on drugs, Akhil Gupta, 'Movimentações globais das colheitas desde a "era das descobertas" e transformações das culturas gastronómicas', in Manuela Ribeiro Sanches (ed.), *Portugal não é um país pequeno. Contar o Império na pós-colonialidade* (Lisbon: Cotovia, 2006), pp. 193–213.

30 Eric Wolf, *Europe and the People without History* (Los Angeles/Berkeley, CA: University of California Press, 1997 [1982]).

31 Eric Williams, *Capitalism and Slavery* (Chapel Hill, NC: University of North Carolina Press, 1947); Gilroy, *The Black Atlantic*.

32 Doreen Massey, 'A Place Called Home?', *New Formations* 17, 1997, pp. 3–15; Massey, *For Space*.

33 Lila Abu-Lughod, 'Writing against Culture,' in R.G. Fox (ed.), *Recapturing Anthropology: Working in the Present* (Santa Fe, NM: School of American Research Press: Distributed by the University of Washington Press, 1991), pp. 137–62; Gupta and Ferguson, 'Beyond Culture'.

34 Stolcke, 'New Boundaries'.

35 Gilroy, *The Black Atlantic*.

36 The Map of Southern Africa, held in the Portuguese National Library.

37 Valentim Alexandre, 'Ruptura e estruturação de um novo império', in Francisco Bethencourt and Kirti Chaudhuri (eds), *'Configurações políticas'. História da expansão portuguesa.* Vol. 4. *Do Brasil para África (1808–1930)* (Lisbon: Círculo dos Leitores, 1998), pp. 10–211.

38 Created by Henrique Galvão and held at the Portuguese National Library.

39 Robert Stam and Ella Shohat, *Unthinking Eurocentrism: Multiculturalism and the Media* (London and New York: Routledge, 1994).

40 Walter Benjamin, 'Über den Begriff der Geschichte', in Rolf Tiedemann and Hermann Schweppenhäuser (eds), *Gesammelte Schriften* (Frankfurt am Main: Suhrkamp, 1991), pp. 693–703.

41 Benedict Anderson, *Imagined Communities: Reflections on the Origin and Spread of Nationalism*, rev. and extended edition (London and New York: Verso, 1991).

42 Max Horkheimer and Theodor W. Adorno, *Dialektik der Aufklärung* (Frankfurt: S. Fischer, 1986).

43 Aimé Césaire, *Discours sur le Colonialisme* (Paris: Présence Africaine, 1995 [1955]).

44 Charles Boxer, *The Portuguese Seaborne Empire (1415–1825)* (London: Hutchinson, 1969).

45 José Ramos Tinhorão, *Os Negros em Portugal. Uma presença silenciosa* (Lisbon: Caminho, 1997); Didier Lahon, *O Negro no coração do império. Uma memória a resgatar. Séculos XV–XIX* (Lisbon: Secretariado Coordenador dos Programas de Educação Multicultural, Casa do Brasil, 1999); Didier Lahon and Maria Cristina Neto, *Os Negros em Portugal. Séculos XVI–XIX* (Lisbon: Comissão Nacional para as Comemorações dos Descobrimentos Portugueses, 1999).

46 Miguel Vale Almeida, *Um Mar da Cor da Terra. 'Raça', Cultura e Política da Identidade* (Oeiras: Celta, 2000).

47 Renato Rosaldo, *Culture and Truth: The Remaking of Social Analysis*, 2nd edn with a new introduction (Boston: Beacon Press, 1993).

48 Georg Simmel, 'Der Fremde', in Michael Landmann (ed.), *Das Individuelle Gesetz* (Frankfurt am Main: Suhrkamp, 1969), pp. 63–70.

49 Ranajit Guha, 'The Prose of Counter-Insurgency,' in Ranajit Guha and Gayatri Chakravorty Spivak (eds), *Selected Subaltern Studies* (Oxford: Oxford University Press, 1988), pp. 37–86; Gyan Prakash, 'Post-colonial Criticism and Indian Historiography', *Social Text* 31/32, 1992, pp. 8–19; Gayatri Chakravorty Spivak, 'Subaltern Studies: Deconstructing Historiography', in Ranajit Guha and Gayatri Chakravorty Spivak (eds), *Selected Subaltern Studies* (Oxford: Oxford University Press, 1988), pp. 3–32; Gayatri Chakravorty Spivak, *A Critique of Postcolonial Reason: Toward a History of the Vanishing Present* (Cambridge, MA: Harvard University Press, 1999); Dipesh Chakrabarty, *Provincializing Europe: Postcolonial Thought and Historical Difference* (Princeton, NJ: Princeton University Press, 2000).

50 Iain Chambers and Lidia Curti, *The Post-Colonial Question: Common Skies, Divided Horizons* (London and New York: Routledge, 1996).

51 Gilroy, *After Empire*.

52 Edouard Glissant, *Le Discours antillais* (Paris: Seuil, 1981).

53 Chakrabarty, *Provincializing Europe*.

54 Abu Lughod, 'Writing against Culture'.

55 Edouard Glissant, *Traité du tout-monde* (Paris: Gallimard, 1997).

56 Edward W. Said, *Culture and Imperialism* (New York: Vintage, 1994).

57 Chakrabarty, *Provincializing Europe*.

58 Glissant, *Traité du tout-monde*, p. 31. 'La pensée archipélique convient à l'allure de nos mondes. Elle en emprunte l'ambigu, le fragile, le dérivé. Elle consent à la pratique du détour, qui n'est pas fuite ni renoncement. Elle reconnaît la portée des imaginaires de la Trace, qu'elle ratifie. Est-ce là renoncer à se gouverner? Non, c'est s'accorder à ce qui du monde est diffusé en archipels précisément, ces sortes de diversités dans l'étendue, qui pourtant rallient des rives et marient des horizons. Nous nous apercevons de ce qu'il y avait de continental, d'épais et qui pesait dur nous, dans les somptueuses pensées de système qui jusqu'à ce jour ont régi l'Histoire des humanités, et qui ne sont plus adéquates à nos éclatements, à nos histoires ni a nos non moins somptueuses errances. La pensée de l'archipel, des archipels, nous ouvre ces mers.'

Translated by John Elliott

Distance and Mobility: Towards a New Understanding of Modernism*

MING TIAMPO

The history of modernism in art is notoriously Eurocentric, with an unapologetic assertion of centre as its historical subject, and periphery as its Other, its object of inspiration. Even in our contemporary moment, with the increasing pressures of globalisation and multiculturalism, narratives about the period from 1890–1964 that we generally take as the defining dates of modernism remain unchanged. This despite the awareness in contemporary art studies that art is produced around the world, and that discourses of artistic production are interconnected. The history of modernism continues to construct the subject of art history as Euro-American, and the non-western world as the site of modernism's dissemination, or the object of modernism's desire.

The 2006 Tate Artist Timeline (twentieth century), both a publication sold in their bookshop and a mural that frames the gallery spaces for visitors, makes this problem very clear.[1] While prominent artists from the non-western world such as Cai Guo-Qiang,

* An expanded and reworked version of this essay appears as Chapter 2 in *Gutai: Decentering Modernism* (Chicago: University of Chicago Press, forthcoming 2010).

Mona Hatoum, Takashi Murakami and Yinka Shonibare figure prominently at the end of the timeline, the period from 1890–1964 resists internationalisation, even under the pressure of a contemporary globalism seeking progenitors. In the period before 1964, we find few non-western artists, diasporic or otherwise.

Of the non-western artists that are included, the Gutai group, Yayoi Kusama and On Kawara, all active in the 1950s and 1960s, are curiously postdated, with Gutai and Kusama located around 1980, in the performance art cluster, and Kawara in 1970, in the conceptual art cluster, both of which are dated according to milestones in the western canon. Thus, despite their priority in the history of art, these artists are rendered as secondary offshoots to a narrative of western art that is naturalised as universal.

However, modernism was not characterised by Euro-American insularity, but by the consequences of colonialism, imperialism, war, tourism, trade, media and immigration. The question we must ask of art history and of all cultural history is thus, 'Can there be modernism without the Other?' I read this question in two ways: First, did modernism ever exist as a purely western phenomenon? And second, is it possible to conceive of an interculturality that negotiates the distance between self and other so that western and non-western modernism become a part of the same dialogical history? Of course, once we admit that modernism was not just about the West's experience of the Other, but rather about human exchanges that took place in what Mary Louise Pratt calls contact zones, what we think of as modernism must fundamentally change. To the experience of the city, and the promises of technology, for example, we must consider questions of distance and mobility as some of modernism's central preoccupations.

With its clear-cut assertion of centre – be it Paris before World War II or New York after it – modernism was, for artists working outside the metropole, characterised by distance: distance covered by travel, distance spanned by media, distance overcome by communications technology, and most importantly, distance from the centre. Art history has generally assumed that with distance came remoteness from the discipline's main narratives and concerns, characterising artists from the periphery as derivative of the centre.

The evidence from the periphery reveals an entirely different story. My paper today concerns the Gutai group of Japan, for whom working on the margins of the art world was far from being an impediment to innovation. Instead, enhanced awareness of distance provoked by working on the periphery mediated their relation to the centre, allowing the group to use their geographic location to their advantage by stimulating new artistic paradigms and insights. Well aware of the importance of originality in modernist discourse, Gutai used distance (cultural and geographical) as a catalyst for creatively engaging with Euro-America using three strategies that I will touch upon briefly in this paper.

What is fascinating about this group is that their work,[2] such as Murakami Saburō's *Passing Through* (1956), a work in which the artist leapt through twenty-one paper screens, literally breaking through boundaries with his simultaneous act of destruction and creation, pre-dated experiments in what would later be called performance art, installation, and earth art in Euro-America. Despite the important and unprecedented nature of their work, they still continue to be characterised as peripheral to the history of art. Even just recently, art history's most important update to the pedagogical canon, *Art Since 1900*, featured their work in a chapter on non-western modernism entitled the 'dissemination of modernist art through the media and its reinterpretation by artists outside the United States and Europe'.[3]

Clearly, modernism continues to be a politicised story of invention and origins at the centre disseminated to the periphery. Despite their chronological priority in performance art, earth art and installation and thus their critical importance to modernism's so-called march of progress, Gutai artists are characterised as producing – and here I quote again from *Art Since 1900* – 'competent yet rather provincial versions of European' art.[4]

The main question that we must ask in response is what constitutes originality? How is Gutai derivative of Jackson Pollock, but Pollock not derivative of Wassily Kandinsky or André Masson? What is the difference between derivation and family resemblance? Finally, and most importantly, is it possible to move beyond analytical terms such as originality, influence and derivation that remain embroiled in discourses of domination?

That language can be found, rather ironically, in conservative literary critic Harold Bloom's reflections on influence and originality in *The Anxiety of Influence* (1973).[5] In this paper, I will use the tools that he sharpened for defending the western canon to find space for mapping modernism beyond Euro-America.

For Bloom, all authors are afflicted with what he playfully calls influenza; even the greats are entangled in a web of influence with their predecessors. Recognising that originality is never truly a *tabula rasa*, Bloom creates six categories of analysis to describe more precisely the interpoetic relations between poets. Going beyond the black-and-white terms of either derivation or originality, he creates a vocabulary for describing shades of grey. For Bloom, for example, *clinamen* describes a poem that seeks to correct a precursor poem, and *tessera* describes one that completes its precursor antithetically.

The logic that Bloom employs to describe intra-poetic relations between poets within the western tradition can be easily used to conceptualise the interpoetic relations between artists from nominally different traditions when they enter into dialogue. The point of this distinction is not to entrench the boundaries of cultural differences, but simply to acknowledge that differences do exist, even when the distinctions between them are fluid and constantly transgressed. For artists working between traditions, between narratives and across national borders, relations with their predecessors are both interpoetic and intra-poetic. To Bloom's strategies of intra-poetic reading, I thus add three strategies of interpoetic reading that capitalise on the creative potential of perceived distance and mobility that comes with awareness of marginality to understand Gutai experimental work and to serve as a model for other peripheral modernisms: translation, re-contextualisation and quantisation.

Translation: Gutai Experimental Art and Jackson Pollock

Much has already been said about the power of invention through translation, not least by Arjun Appadurai, whose work on the

South Asian translation of cricket into a sport that the British now lose is a prime example.

I will therefore not dwell for long on the question of cultural translation in Gutai. Suffice it to say that the Gutai reception of American artist Jackson Pollock through Yoshihara's large library of national and international art journals formed the foundations of a creative relationship that could not possibly be characterised as derivative. Rather, the translations and transformations that took place in their dialogue with Pollock enabled them to make work that was both innovative and relevant to the most important debates of the centre.

Whereas American artists and critics saw Pollock pushing up against the limitations of the medium of painting, Gutai saw his work as calling for an expansion of that medium. In particular, they saw the photographs of him in his studio taken by Hans Namuth as a provocation to question the sanctity of the picture plane. Situated at the crossroads of three artistic traditions, European, American and Japanese, Gutai was well placed to understand the problematics of painting within the Euro-American context without being bound by its constraints. When considered in the context of American art, Gutai's self-conscious redefinition of painting was a radical notion, and quite the opposite of Clement Greenberg's argument emphasising the flatness of painting, claiming that 'purity in art consists in the acceptance, willing acceptance of the limitations of the medium of the specific art'.[6]

Rather than accepting the limitations of the medium, they extended them, making works that they considered moving paintings in time and space, such as Tanaka Atsuko's 1957 work *Stage Clothes*, in which her body became the canvas itself, through which and on which forms and colours were manifest as she removed layers of clothing, unravelling new garments from the hems of previous costumes and reconstructing dresses from the sleeves of others. The performance concluded with her famous *Electric Dress*, a costume made of coloured lightbulbs that blinked as figures wearing the dresses walked around on stage, glowing eerily. Breaking with the Euro-American definition of painting, Gutai rejected the claim of Pollock's universality and rendered his project contingent upon the European 'modern system of the arts' and Clement Greenberg's purism. Using translation as a strategy of interpoetic interpretation, Gutai thus radically opened up painting to include space and time with their experiments outdoors and on the stage.

Re-contextualisation: Gutai Experimental Art and *Matsuri*

Re-contextualisation is perhaps the most widespread strategy of creative interpretation employed by artists and writers from the margins. It is also the strategy most easily assimilated by the dominant narrative of modernism, easily read as exotic. Re-contextualisation is simply the use of context-specific concepts, forms, narratives or materials from the artist's context of origin in a different context, such as international modernism.

In its commonest form, re-contextualisation used the discursive space opened by primitivism, *Japonisme* and other exoticisms to initiate dialogue with international modernism. For many artists, writers and intellectuals seeking to enter into dialogue with Europe, such as Léopold Sédar Senghor of Senegal, Abanindranath Tagore of India and Morita Shiryū of Japan, these discourses of exoticism were the only certain means to achieve what Morita called 'world relevance'.[7] Realising the importance of Japanese calligraphy for Euro-American modernists such as Franz Kline, for example, Morita sought to put contemporary calligraphy in dialogue with Abstract Expressionism by creating highly simplified calligraphic works, made for 'non-character-reading nations'.

Re-contextualisation can also take place less strategically, whenever artists draw from their immediate cultural environments to enrich, inspire and inform their work. As Pollock was embedded in his own context, so too was Gutai. Envisioning the art world as interconnected and layered, Gutai drew inspiration from both its local and global contexts. In addition to its engagement with the discourses, techniques and debates of the international art world, Gutai also situated its work with respect to the Japanese art world as well as its context of everyday life. In particular, Gutai's drive towards the everyday, their use of non-art materials and experi-

ments with site-specificity encouraged a high degree of engagement with their local context. Thus, just as Pollock drew from
Native American sources and American jazz, Gutai made work
that consciously drew from Japanese cultural forms.

When, for example, Gutai artists responded to the photographs
of Jackson Pollock painting with an expansion of painting to
include time and space, their works drew from a vocabulary of
cultural expression that surrounded them, and that continues to
persist today: Japanese festivals. These festivals, or *matsuri*,
provided not just a generalised ambiance for the outdoor exhibitions, but also an iconography, a conceptual understanding of the
relationship between man and nature, a framework for theorising
the almost animistic view of materials espoused by Gutai, and a
model for the role of art in life.

Matsuri are Shinto or Shinto-Buddhist purification festivals,
which continue to take place several hundred times a year in urban
as well as rural places all over Japan. They are intended to renew
ties with the deities, called *kami*, as well as with nature, and also
serve to renew bonds between individuals in a community. Unlike
in art exhibitions, where boundaries are enforced between viewer,
object, artist and curator, in *matsuri* boundaries are systematically
broken down to create a space of freedom. Otherworldly events,
bridging the space between the natural and the supernatural,
matsuri open up a domain of freedom and play beyond rationality
in which normal modes of social interaction are suspended.

In addition to providing a perspective on the relationship
between the human spirit and the material, as well as a model for
creative community events in outdoor spaces, *matsuri* were a rich
source of visual vocabulary for Gutai artists. Shiraga Kazuo's
Challenging Mud (1955) drew, for example, from the yearly *Doronko
Matsuri* or mud festivals that take place every spring prior to the
rice-planting season, and Motonaga Sadamasa's *Fune* (1956) drew
from the common practice of *okuribi*, sending *kami* back to their
otherworldly homes by floating candlelit lanterns down the rivers
and back to the ocean.

Gutai's use of *matsuri* as material for their artwork was just one
of many sources that they used to create multilayered works that

were relevant to the international art scene, but also undeniably distinctive. Re-contextualisation thus functioned as a strategy of interpoetic creativity on two levels. First, it was a source of inspiration or raw materials in the *creation* of original works of art. Second, it functioned as an anchor in the *reception* of these works, maintaining Gutai's connection to a context different from that of the putative centre and resisting claims from the centre that this work had its origins in New York or Paris, as Yves Klein asserted in the Chelsea Hotel Manifesto of 1962: 'I speak of that group of Japanese painters who with great refinement used my method in a strange way.'[8]

As with translation, re-contextualisation uses cultural distance from the centre as a source of invention. The final strategy that I will introduce today uses geographical distance as a catalyst.

Quantisation: Gutai Experimental Art and Gutai Portables

In an article from 6 January 2008, *New York Times* art critic Holland Cotter posed the following question: 'When you have YouTube at your disposal, who needs Chelsea?'[9] He went on to describe a generation of artists who no longer feel the need to physically locate themselves in the art world's centres of gravity. Working from Texas to Sweden, they use the Internet to access the rest of the art world. In the process, these artists are reimagining both the structure of the art world and the form of the art object. No longer subject to the politics and preferences of New York's gallery system, they are decentring the art world by taking the power of production and distribution away from New York. The mediascape that they are constructing, however, has its own internal logic that demands the digital compliance of all works that it distributes.

Artists working on the geographical margins of the art world have often used media technology, what Marshall McLuhan calls 'extensions of man', to access larger audiences and reach for centres of power.[10] The changes wrought upon art, and upon the art world, have been quite radical, ranging from the invention of portable painting formats to the dematerialisation of the work of art. I call this process of rendering the artwork more portable and more easily disseminated quantisation, after the digital operation of making image files compressible and expandable, typically to facilitate distribution. One of the most radical changes to the art object in our generation, it was first explored by artists on the periphery, aware of their distance from the centre.

Gutai quantised its work on many levels to cope with the challenges of distance and to interact with a broader art world using the international postal network. They explored innovative ways of using the *Gutai* journal as a method of dissemination, and also created an early form of mail art in the form of postcard-sized exhibitions that were shipped to mailboxes around the world. The strategies they used to make what I call Gutai portables provided room for invention, encouraging new ways of thinking about the display, production and status of the work of art. Of particular note are the group's preparations for their participation in the *Nul 1965* exhibition organised by Dutch artist Henk Peeters at the Stedelijk Museum in Amsterdam. This show marked a turning point for the group's strategies of quantisation, shifting from the creation of transportable works of art to a reconsideration of the art object's very nature, from material to concept.

In planning for an exhibition where the artists could not be present for the installation, quantisation opened a space of creativity, as the artist's hand receded in importance and was replaced by concept. A cogent example of this evolution is seen in the case of Yoshida Toshio, whose early production was the epitome of the stated Gutai relationship between artist and material. For example, his 1955 *Work 55-7* is a single painted gesture incarnated in material. The heavy impasto does not so much represent as it embodies, and the combination of white on black makes oblique reference to the calligraphic tradition, where the artist's mind is lodged in the trace of the brush.

In his proposal for *Nul 1965*, entitled *Semi-Automatic Drip Circle*, Yoshida withdrew the artist's hand almost completely, designing a 'semi-automatic' work that would have operated without the artist's intervention, and thereby enabled painting at a distance. The drawing called for two dripping cans of paint, one red, one black, to be attached to an inverted V-shaped structure that was suspended from a tree over a 3.6-metre-square canvas. At each end, where the paint cans were hung, was a sail used to catch the wind and spin the apparatus, which would, over time, create a red and black dripped circle on the canvas below. Anticipating Sol LeWitt's 1967 comment about Conceptual Art that 'the idea becomes a machine that makes the art',[11] this unrealised work opened the door for Yoshida's most successful series of automatic sculptures in the 1960s.

For the young Nasaka Senkichirō, the far-away exhibition provided an impetus to dream up wild, implausible conceptual projects. In a gesture that foreshadowed Gutai's later interest in space technology, *Rocket Tape Show* was a plan to attach lengths of coloured tape to rockets, which would have been shot into the air to create an ephemeral drawing in space – an almost completely conceptual work.

Nasaka was not the only artist to be inspired by new technologies. Demonstrating the centrality of media and dissemination to his thinking, Kanayama submitted a proposal for a television in which the sound and picture were not synchronised, a comment perhaps on the instantaneity of global culture engendered through television, which nevertheless was somewhat lost in translation. Had it been realised, this work would have been contemporaneous with Nam June Paik's earliest television experiments.

In the context of the late 1960s, the privileging of idea over material had an additional resonance with the emergence of global conceptualism and the rise of concept-based art that could be packed up in a suitcase, sent on a postcard, or performed by an artist in transit.[12] Indeed, placing the quantisation of Gutai art in the framework of 1960s conceptualism gives us new insight into the group's work as a harbinger of the dematerialisation of the work of art that climaxed in the late 1960s.[13] Situated far from the putative centres and coping with the problem of distance from an extremely early date, Gutai was, in retrospect, a leader in early conceptualist tendencies, employing quantisation as a strategy to creatively open up significant possibilities and usher in a new era of artmaking that overcame great distances in a rapidly shrinking world.

Conclusion

I would like to end here with a work by Kanayama, another unrealised proposal for the *Nul 1965* exhibition. The drawing shows a hand holding a stamped letter coming out of a mailbox, a visual metaphor for the Gutai portion of the exhibition, which was sent from Japan to Amsterdam as a pile of flattened works, consisting of unstretched canvases and sketches for reconstruction. Kanayama's proposal made explicit reference to the changes being made to the work of art in the age of transnational dissemination. It underscored the demands that mobility made to the medium of art, shifting the work away from material to concept and documentation. Labelled in English, the work also pointed to the growing importance of English as a lingua franca by 1965, and to the translations made to the work of art itself as it moved from country to country and medium to medium. Finally, the stamp from the country of origin on the top right side of the envelope, an item of both fetishistic and philatelic interest, linked the deterritorialised letter back to its home country and explored the meaning and significance of place and context, even within the postal system's global networks.

Bringing together Gutai's strategies of translation, re-contextualisation and quantisation, the work reveals how aware artists on the periphery were of their distance from the centre, and demonstrates the creative potential that distance brought to their work.

Notes

1 The Tate Artist Timeline (twentieth century) can be accessed online in the portfolio of the designer Sara Fanelli's website: www.sarafanelli. com (accessed 14 January 2009). It should be noted that Fanelli designed the timeline, but had no input regarding its contents.

2 This and many other Gutai works discussed in this paper can be consulted online at www.gutai.com.

3 Hal Foster, Rosalind Krauss, Yve-Alain Bois and Benjamin Buchloh, *Art Since 1900: Modernism, Antimodernism, Postmodernism* (New York: Thames & Hudson, 2004), p. 373.

4 Ibid.

5   Harold Bloom, *The Anxiety of Influence* (Oxford: Oxford University Press, 1973).

6   Clement Greenberg, 'Towards a Newer Laocoön' (1940); reprinted in Francis Frascina (ed.), *Pollock and After: The Critical Debate*, 2nd edn (New York: Routledge, 2000), p. 66. It is very unlikely that Yoshihara was conscious of Greenberg's writings on painting in the crucial period of the early 1950s. His archives contain little evidence of Greenberg in the 1950s, and Greenberg was not available in Japanese until 'Modernist Painting' was first translated in 1963, and *Art and Culture* was translated in 1965. For more on Greenberg's reception in Japan, see Kenji Kajiya, 'Gosadō suru buki: Kuremento Gurinbāgu, bunka reisen, gurōbarizeshon' [Malfunctioning weapon: Clement Greenberg, the cultural cold war, and globalisation], *Amerika kenkyu* 37, 2003, pp. 83–105.

7   Elizabeth Harney, *In Senghor's Shadow* (Durham, NC: Duke University Press, 2004); Partha Mitter, *The Triumph of Modernism* (Chicago: University of Chicago Press, 2007); and Bert Winther-Tamaki, *Art in the Encounter of Nations* (Honolulu: University of Hawaii Press, 2001).

8   Yves Klein, 'Chelsea Hotel Manifesto', exh. cat. (New York: Alexander Iolas Gallery, 1962); reprinted in Gilbert Perlein and Bruno Corà (eds), *Yves Klein: Long Live the Immaterial*, exh. cat. (Nice: Musée d'art moderne et d'art contemporain / Prato: Museo Pecci, 2000), pp. 85–88.

9   Holland Cotter, 'Video Art Thinks Big: That's Showbiz', *New York Times*, 6 January 2008, AR18.

10 Marshall McLuhan, *Understanding Media: The Extensions of Man* (New York: McGraw-Hill, 1964).

11 Sol LeWitt, 'Paragraphs on Conceptual Art', *Artforum* 5.10, June 1967, pp. 79–84; reprinted in Alexander Alberro and Blake Stimson (eds), *Conceptual Art: A Critical Anthology* (Cambridge and London: MIT Press, 1999), p. 12. I owe this reference to Nicole Neufeld.

12 For more on global conceptualism, see *Global Conceptualism: Points of Origin 1950s–1980s*, exh. cat. (New York: Queens Museum of Art, 1999). For Japanese conceptualism in particular, see Reiko Tomii, 'Concerning the Institution of Art: Conceptualism in Japan', in *Global Conceptualism*, pp. 15–30.

13 Lucy Lippard, *Six Years: The Dematerialization of the Art Object from 1966 to 1972* (New York: Praeger, 1973).

Europe and Islam: Shared History, Shared Identity, Shared Destiny

MUSTAPHA TLILI

Let me first paint in brushstrokes the contours of the grand narrative. Before there was 'The West', there was Christianity and Christendom. From the time of Muhammad's prophecy, Islam found itself in constant interaction with Christianity, with which it shared a strong kinship. However, the ambitions of the 'new kid on the block' – the block being Abrahamic monotheism – created tensions between the three faiths and led to territorial expansion by Muhammad's successors – caliphs and dynastic rulers: the Umayyads, the Abassids and the Ottomans.

Except for a short interruption resulting from the Battle of Poitiers (Tours) in 732, most of the lands of the Christianised – and by this time crumbling – Roman empire, in both its geographically western and eastern versions, gradually fell under the authority of Islam until the failed siege of Vienna in 1683. How did this history affect the development of European/western identity?

'The West' developed as a self-conscious identity throughout Europe in the late Dark Ages. Until then, there had been no single identity unifying the tribes of the lands ruled by Islam since 712, when Muslim soldiers first landed on the shores of Iberia (or, al-Andalus, for Muslims). Therefore, European identity was born out of confrontation and interaction with the new dominant power and its civilisation — Islam. A shared history of short battles and protracted wars (including the Crusades), of commerce, diplomatic relations, cultural exchanges, and marriages slowly shaped this new European identity and provided the ingredients — in science, philosophy, literature, poetry, architecture, music, fashion, and cuisine — that sparked the European Renaissance and the exploration of distant shores.

Since the tragedy of September 11th, we have witnessed a new interest among historians in highlighting this shared identity, which links Islam and the West at a much deeper level than reflected by the simplistic 'clash of civilisations' theory concocted by Samuel Huntington. Three books in particular merit attention: Maria Rose Menocal's *The Ornament of the World: How Muslims, Jews, and Christians Created a Culture of Tolerance in Medieval Spain*; Michael Hamilton Morgan's *Lost History: The Enduring Legacy of Muslim Scientists, Thinkers and Artists*; and David Levering Lewis's *God's Crucible: Islam and the Making of Europe, 570–1215*.[1] These three books brilliantly challenge the glaring ignorance of the 'clash of civilisations' theory advanced by the neo-conservatives to justify their political and military agenda since the end of the Cold War.

Beyond demonstrating the hollowness of its core arguments, which contradict the historical record, any critique of the 'clash of civilisations' theory should unveil its hidden political agenda. The same can be said of Lyon University's Professor Sylvain Gouguenheim's *Aristote au Mont Saint-Michel: Les racines grecques de l'Europe chrétienne*,[2] which claims that Muslim scholars could not have assimilated Greek rationalism and transmitted its legacy to Europe, given Islam's incapacitating submission to divine authority. For Professor Gouguenheim, the Renaissance owes its advent to the monks of the Norman bastion of Saint-Michel — of what is now Normandy. According to him, and contrary to the universally accepted historical record, it is the monks of Saint-Michel who restored the lost corpus of classical antiquity to the West, long before Arab scholars mastered Aristotle, Plato, Ptolemy and Euclid.

Intellectual debate matters. It allows us to contextualise the onslaught of current events, particularly at a time when individuals and policymakers can find themselves dangerously overwhelmed with the unrelenting flow of information in a globalised world. Yes – words and concepts can be as powerful as the sword. Images and perceptions have real consequences. Since the end of the Cold War, the frantic search for a new enemy to replace communism has led some in the West to spin revisionist histories and inflammatory concepts to justify hegemonic policies, military aggression and other means of domination. We know the results. The Iraq War is a gigantic disaster. We should remember that Bernard Lewis[3] was a frequent visitor to the Bush White House.

Islam has moved to the forefront of world affairs. Although the Islamic world today may appear chaotic, confusing and sometimes even menacing, its importance is undeniable, and its relationship with the rest of the world may be the defining issue of our times.

It is easy to judge each side by its extremists: the radical Islamists on one side, and on the other, the neo-conservatives and the Evangelical Right in the United States and the Far Right in Europe. These vocal but unrepresentative minorities have dominated the public conversation since September 11th, each of them offering a polarised version of history that can lead only to catastrophe for all, if not checked by a counter-narrative based on historical fact and implemented in terms of wise policies.

Is conflict between Islam and the West inevitable? The answer is clearly in our hands, to a large extent. Given its shared history with Islam, Europe can play a critical role in shaping this answer. Today, Islam is in Europe again. There are 25 million Muslim Europeans, who consider themselves Muslims *of* Europe – not Muslims *in* Europe. They contribute significantly to the economic welfare and cultural vitality of the continent and are, by any measure, a critical asset for Europe's success in a highly competitive century. Europe needs its Muslim citizens today. It will need them even more tomorrow, to satisfy its demands in terms of labour, population growth, and to respond to challenges of the future.

For the most part, however, although they live in immediate proximity to non-Muslim European citizens, recent social science studies attest that these European Muslim communities remain at a regrettable political, economic and social distance from the mainstream. In addition, today's European Muslims find themselves facing the challenge of 'integration' into the only society they know: Europe. Meanwhile, no one, from the European Union to the popular media, has been able to define what constitutes 'integration' with any degree of precision or clarity. Isn't it time for Europe to change the terms of the debate? Isn't it time to offer up a new paradigm that clearly defines the public rights and obligations of every European, Muslim and non-Muslim alike? What Europe needs is a citizenship pact, linking the individual to the state and to his community without interference in personal beliefs, values, or other aspects of personal identity. The experience of the United States has proven that citizenship is the bedrock of common destiny.

In order to prevent the alienation that frequently leads to radicalisation and sometimes violence, all those concerned – governments, cultural associations, employers, educational institutions, faith leaders and others – should band together to develop what I have called in other forums a 'new citizenship pact' that would reassure Europe's Muslim citizens of their right to their private beliefs and values, as long as their public behaviour is in accordance with the legal systems and civic cultures of their new countries.

As full citizens of Europe, European Muslims could become an inspiration for the larger Muslim world as it struggles to strike a balance between faith, tradition and modernity. This could in turn lead to a more peaceful and productive relationship between the Muslim world and the West.

Education, both formal – through academic programmes and textbooks – and informal – through public intellectual interventions, the philanthropic contributions of non-profit organisations and through information dissemination by the media – can also play a significant role in conflict resolution. We need to educate the Other, to educate western public opinion and western policymakers about the complexities of 'Islam', about the frustrations, aspirations and needs of 1.5 billion Muslims in more than fifty countries; and educate Islamic public opinion and Islamic policy-makers about the West's longing for security and peace, and desire to understand.

The alternative? I happen to be a novelist, and find in the realm of literary imagination the power of the 'seer', to use Arthur Rimbaud's word – a power that allows me to probe man's fate beyond the limits of reality or conventional wisdom. At the request of my Parisian publisher, Gallimard, which wanted to bring out my very first novel, *La Rage aux tripes* (Gut Anger), in a twentieth anniversary edition, I revisited in 1995 the journey of my main character and caught up with him in his defeat, living in exile in Manhattan, after wandering the Islamic world for more than twenty years, from one tragedy to another: from Palestine to Bosnia to the civil war in Algeria. My protagonist, Jalal Ben Chérif, a legendary commander of Algeria's war of liberation against France, and now a disillusioned man selling real estate in New York, is interviewed by a French journalist. The 'interview' appears in the paperback edition of the novel as a sort of epilogue to a story that started at the beginning of Algeria's struggle for inde-pendence. Here is a passage from that interview, in rough translation kindly provided by my friend, Columbia University Professor Richard Bulliet:

Jalal Ben Chérif:
... It's simply that I *see*. At the same time that I see the idiots for Allah do what they do in Gaza, Algiers, or Tehran ... I see these tens of thousands of Muslim women and children being slaugh-tered with obscene indifference by the disciples of Hegel and Voltaire and the other heralds of civilisation and of human rights. And I remember ...
    I remember Grenada in 1492 and other rivers of blood. And I ask myself whether the sons and grandsons of peasants, the radical idiots for God then, are as crazy as we tend to think they are in their implacable determination to cleanse the world

of any trace of the bastards, the fifth column, including your humble servant, who is living in exile in New York for the rest of his life. Their ultimate goal is apparently to let loose, or should I say take up again, the Great Battle interrupted in 1492.

Journalist:
1492?

Jalal Ben Chérif:
Yes, 1492. The fall of Granada at the end of eight centuries of power and grandeur. You must understand that I, Jalal Ben Chérif, have fought to avenge my family, my mother, burnt alive by the French, not for some grand design. Like Camus did in choosing his mother over justice. I am afraid that the real gut anger, fuelled by the memory of all the humiliations inflicted on Islam by the West since Granada, is what enflames the soul, the heart and the spirit of these soldiers in the Great Battle. Mine, ours, our anger at ourselves, we bastards of 'wars of independence' and other famous 'national liberations', this anger is trivial compared with the new and terrible fire that is consuming the lands of Islam today. Rage and blood for a great battle, I call it ...

Journalist:
You talk as if all this was inevitable.

Jalal Ben Chérif:
Think about that little skirmish between Communism and the West that lasted for seventy-five years. It was nothing more than that, a skirmish. Nothing more. A family quarrel, so to speak, that caused some damage, but then in the end everything returned to normal. Yesterday's cruel tyrants have become virtuous democrats today. The nice western family had regained its harmony, its rationality and its benign ideas; and everyone again swears by the same gods, and the same founding fathers: Voltaire, Montesquieu, Hegel, and a few others. Even Marx will end up being disinfected one day, and he too will take

his place again in the family pantheon, venerated and cherished, as he was in the past. Derrida has already begun to rehabilitate him, and I'm willing to bet that Jean-François Lyotard won't be far behind. Believe me, the true battle against the West is the Great Battle of the Year III of Islam, 503 years after the fall of Granada, the last Andalusian kingdom, which ushered in the Age of Humiliation.

Journalist:
Do you mean that the true enemy of the West is Islam? That one or the other will always dominate at every moment of history? Be clear, what you are saying is very serious.

Jalal Ben Chérif:
It's too soon to say, but the beginnings are there and very disturbing. Never has the violence been so ferocious, on both sides, whether in words or in blood. It's the same thing …

The real and sole truth, undeniable and absolutely irrefutable – and so ignoble – is that, the West doesn't give a damn. What do I mean? That it basks in the idea that for a few more years it can hold Islam's head under water, stifle it whenever it tries hopelessly to breathe, and then, the next day, throw itself entirely into the Great Battle, led today only by a few hotheads of Year III in the Aurès and in Egypt and some others in Turkey.

Journalist:
It is too late? Is all this, this idiocy, irreversible?

Jalal Ben Chérif:
I ask myself that … The Great Battle against the West may eventually have the virtue of cleaning the landscape of the boils caused by five centuries of humiliation and thereby laying the groundwork for some indispensable future reconciliation. But we may still have to pass through tears, and blood, and misunderstandings, and tragedies.

Journalist:

It's astonishing how up-to-date you are on western thought, which you continue quite remarkably to demonstrate, especially considering that you spend so much of your life these days in real estate. You seem to be *au courant* of the most recent ideas — Derrida, Lyotard ...

Jalal Ben Chérif:

Do you mean that I'm irredeemable because of my extreme fantasies? This is very probably, indeed certainly, what my friends in Algeria think, whom disrespectful attitudes like mine can only disturb. In the face of their sole truth, I assert the primacy of doubt, of the beauty of thought, of the pleasure of knowing and the taste for happiness, which is the goal of such adventures of the spirit. Believe me, the choice for a Muslim today is not whether to be on the side of Salman Rushdie and his deplorably casual way of offending the sensibility and culture of more than a billion believers, or on that of Hassan Turabi, the petty dictator theoretician of Khartoum who has contributed to giving Islam a reputation as hell on earth — though certainly not the Córdoba, Seville and Granada of my ancestors, the Ben Chérifs, during their centuries of glory and splendour. In those days the barbarous princes of Europe sent their embassies to our emirs and caliphs to beg for a little science, and culture, and rationality. Avicenna, Averroës, al-Farabi and others could think freely about choices, about all sorts of alternatives. They could ask questions and make the sole limit of their thought the power to think further and deeper, even about the most sacred taboos. Today, alas, on every subject they stupidly cite the Qur'ān because they are incapable of understanding anything beyond it. At the same time they wield a knife in their other hand, ready to cut someone's throat, or put assassins on your trail with a *fatwa*. I tell you this: I see only blood on the horizon, blood everywhere, without end ...

Notes

1 Maria Rose Menocal, *The Ornament of the World: How Muslims, Jews, and Christians Created a Culture of Tolerance in Medieval Spain* (Boston, MA: Little, Brown and Co., 2002); Michael Hamilton Morgan, *Lost History: The Enduring Legacy of Muslim Scientists, Thinkers and Artists* (New York: Random House, 2007); and David Levering Lewis, *God's Crucible: Islam and the Making of Europe, 570–1215* (New York: W.W. Norton, 2008).

2 Sylvain Gouguenheim, *Aristote au Mont Saint-Michel: Les racines grecques de l'Europe chrétienne* (Paris: Editions du Seuil, 2008).

3 British-American historian, Orientalist, and political commentator Bernard Lewis is a widely-read expert on the Middle East, and is regarded as one of the West's leading scholars of that region. His advice has been frequently sought by policymakers, including the former Bush administration. (Source: Wikipedia)

Time to Listen to the 'Other' while the "Other" still Exists, before All That's Left is the *Other...*

Or

A Neo-animist Pre-manifesto

RUY DUARTE DE CARVALHO

... since I'm civically, emotionally and intellectually a part of the general category of the Other in relation to Europe, the question of the Other, on the other hand, given the phenotypical conditions and origin that I have, has also always been part of my existential and personal experience within the actual African and Angolan context in which I have led my life and plied my trade ... this has led me, in order to see if I can manage to understand the world and to understand myself with it and within it, to identify and recognise a multiplicity of Others ... in the present case I shall only mention three categories of the Other, which are the ones that seem to me to be capable of allowing me to try to explain what I may have to say here ...

... I shall consider here as the *Other*, in italics, those individuals and groups, many of whom were either already born or were produced in the territories of the ex-metropolises either from ex-colonised parents or from parents who came from the ex-colonies and who today, through the full application of their rights under statute law, belong to the national populations of these same ex-metropolises, even though they are recognised as different from the predominant mass by virtue of their phenotypical or cultural features …

… as the 'Other', between single inverted commas, the westernised ex-colonised people with whom the West deals in the contexts of the ex-colonies

… and finally as the "Other", between double inverted commas, those who are marked by features associated with populations such that, despite belonging as nationals to nation states that exist today based on the boundaries drawn up under the system of ex-colonies, they still maintain customs, practices and behaviours that are more akin to precolonial rather than postcolonial or more or less westernised contexts … in other words, there still exists, in many cases, an "Other" who is not, or not yet completely, westernised … who, in the course of a present time that is also our own, obviously continues to be subject to a westernising pressure that ends up being the dominant feature of the daily life shared by people who, in the light of the much proclaimed human rights, are worth just as much as any other people in the world …

… it's just that their situation and condition are so greatly differentiated in the national contexts within which they exist that, in the same way as here in Europe, where I am currently speaking, the ex-metropolises sometimes seem not to know exactly what to do with the *Other*, in italics, who comes into being in their own territory, so also the 'Other', between single inverted commas, who governs the territories of the ex-colonies, similarly seems, in turn, to have difficulty in knowing what to do with that "Other", between double inverted commas …

… in my view, this is one of the problems, one of the obstacles facing the modern-day world, because of the historical process that has shaped it and continues to preserve it such as it is today, and clearly I am talking about western expansion, such as it has developed and still remains in progress …

… other problems, however, many of which, again in my view, end up being set up or regarded as obstacles, are to be found in today's world precisely as a result, and I insist on this, of western expansion and the place that the western civilisational matrix has ended up imposing on the entire world ... in such a way, in fact, that the evidence of a situation does not therefore cease to pile up and impose itself with ever greater urgency, as is happening right now with the financial crisis that the world is facing ... it seems that the western, and westernised, world decidedly cannot ignore any longer the urgent need to do something previously untried and unheard of by itself ... from what I have repeatedly heard about this matter in recent weeks, all that I can glean is that all the western institutions and governments called upon to express their opinion on the current crisis have found themselves faced with the need to stress that their current predominant concerns with finance must not and cannot hide, ignore or delay the vital global concern with health, and the preservation and saving of the environment of the planet ... and, even further, that the developing countries, which are not exactly the ones that are most immediately called upon to tackle the crisis of the general western and westernised world, demand to be consulted immediately ...

... and, at this point, it occurs to me that I must formulate the following question: since the globalised world recognises that it must urgently do something by itself about the world's global fate, and since the voices of the emerging countries will necessarily have to be listened to, would it not perhaps therefore also be time to heed what all manner of voices that still make up the world may yet have to say in what is perhaps in everybody's interest? Even the voices of that "Other" that I identify here between double inverted commas? That we can live without him, resorting to the theme of this conference, is perhaps possible, if only because he will inexorably disappear, but would it not be pertinent, for the purposes of discussion and for the fate of the world, to try to listen to him while he still exists?

... I am leaving Namibia, where for the last five months I have enjoyed the luxury of being able to dedicate myself exclusively to a book that I am writing ... it is semi-fictional, following on from others in which I have experimented with this genre, and its action mainly takes place in south-west Angola and north-west Namibia, where there still exist precisely those kinds of populations that I can identify with that absolute Other that I have been talking about … when I received the invitation there to take part in this conference, I accepted without any real hesitation because, in my view, I saw myself once again placed in a situation in which reality comes face to face with fiction and considered that I might in some way include the fact of my being here now in the programme that I had previously set for myself and which, because of this, I thus found being interrupted … in the plot that I have been working on in this book in progress, at a certain point, two of its characters consider that, based on local cosmology and cosmogony (of Southern African in this case), they might be able to propose to the world the figure of a guardian hero who is perfectly suited to dealing with the concerns, afflictions and emergencies that seem to require an immediate, effective and appropriate response, and yet, at the same time, one that it is difficult to conjecture or conceive from the world we live in, because these concerns, afflictions and emergencies are after all based on premises and dynamics that the modern world seems, at the same time, little concerned with calling into question …… the hero in question goes under the name of Nambalisita, a figure of great stature in the collective imagination and the expressions of the populations of the region that I referred to and which I also normally tend to identify as a rural, clannish patch of south-western Africa, composed essentially of *herero*, *ovambo* and *nyaneka* populations … Nambalisita, with whom I have been in very close contact ever since more than a quarter of a century ago I shot a film called *Nelisita*, is self-generated … he was born from a self-fertilised egg … and, fighting against evil and all the ills and confusions of the world, Nambalisita calls upon all the animals that he has bred, his brothers, his boys, and even upon the entire animal kingdom itself …… just that, as the characters in my book know full well, it is not easy to propose a hero of this type to the western and westernised world that holds the reins of the world and controls its destinies … Nambalisita emerges from a cosmogonic and cosmological matrix that is not the one which gave the West the power to come and occupy the place that it occupies today in the globalised world … while for us here, at this edge of Africa, as one of these characters says, for our

way of seeing things, every living being has a similar soul, whether
we are talking about people, hyenas or lizards, which is expressed
by living in accordance with the body that it has, one which is the
same for the whites and for those whom the whites converted,
tamed in their own manner, and it is only the body that identifies
man as an animal, because what constitutes him as a man is having
a soul that the rest of the animal world do not ... and that is the
expression of the reason, arrogance and haughtiness of the invader
... it places man outside the biological condition as if he were safe
from such vileness and shared with God the divine condition, only
him and not the rest of creation ... man at the centre of the universe
and serving as a measure for everything, even for God ... the
anthropomorphising of everything, even of God ... the divine
configured as a white god with a white beard ... all tamed
according to a model that even envisaged the savage that we would
be here, a half-human that only has access to the platform of
humanity, is only truly human when measured not in relation to
the rest of the world's creation, but in relation to certain men that
have a version of the world and life that they impose on the others,
and the weapons, equipment and means to derive benefit from this
... the universe is made for their use and, in the name of God and
civilisation, they are meanwhile authorised to convert the whole
world, divine, human, animate and inanimate, in their own ways,
in their own way ... that of the paradigm that covered western
expansion, and so did not commit the sin of overestimating people
... did not place them as high as they should have been ... because
even after the time had come for decolonisation and handing over
the local sovereignties to the westernised members of the previously discovered indigenous populations, what did in fact happen
was that they were bequeathed, without a nation or a pluri-
national arrangement, a poisoned legacy of modern states defined
by colonial political frontiers that are historically recent and alien
to the different and frequently distinct groups or societies who
were either enveloped or divided by them ... and they were
immediately required to perform as nation states in a universal
world in which the predominant regionalities being consummated
within the political framework of globalities are tending, at the

same time, towards ridding themselves of that political figure of the nation state, as is happening, for example, with the European Community ...

... only a great paradigm shift can therefore add another character fully versed in western terminologies ... a shift that is both paradigmatic and truly pragmatic ... but it is one that should not include those opportunistic and cynical pragmatisms in which the category of what is necessary and advantageous has completely replaced that of what is possible, and which consist of not being able to envisage anything without immediately calculating the partial benefit that is inspired by the situation and without looking at the world in any way other than in this light ... ... in the same way it would be necessary to take into account the fact that, in the case of such a paradigm shift, it would not be sufficient just to accept that the "Other" could be capable of seeing the phenomena and the world and assessing them and incorporating them, using them according to his own reasons and interests, as the westerner does... this is not any kind of paradigm shift, it is a question of good sense ... a paradigm shift would be to admit, and to recognise, that someone, even while being the "Other" and thinking in a radically different way, might be able to see certain things and certain phenomena in a better way, one that is more suited to the effective configuration of the world, and that, in this case, it is the western and westernised people who would have to learn from the "Other", and that this would end up suiting everybody's purposes ... a shift, therefore, that would make it possible, in view of the obstacles that the expansion and imposition of the western paradigm raises all over the world – including in those parts of the world from which it came, because they are now left to deal with the change, namely the children of the ex-colonised who are being born there ... a shift that would make it possible for western knowledge itself to consider it time to pay a different kind of attention to the so-called archaic discourses, to devote itself to making a counterdiscovery, so to speak, of those who were previously discovered by the caravels ... which perhaps, in the language of the specialists, might be formulated by saying that it would be time to listen to the 'Other' while the "Other" still exists, before all that's left is the *Other*, that unpredictable universal mestizo that time itself will be responsible for producing ...

... and this is what my characters say in the book that I am writing and that I have interrupted in order to be able to be here now ... that book will shortly be available to everybody, and I shall only talk here now about one of the aspects that I have mentioned: listening to that "Other" while he still exists ... does he still exist?

... yes, he does still exist, in certain parts of the world, such as the one that I am now leaving and which has attracted my total attention for several decades ... and if I commit myself here and now to launching a campaign to ensure that this "Other" is still taken into account and listened to, it is not so much because I believe that we must all go and listen attentively to what the elders of that place may still have to say to us and to teach us ... my experience as an anthropologist leads me to show the greatest possible caution in heeding what today's elders might have to say to those who approach them and question them ... they say exactly what they very pragmatically consider that they want the others to hear, as happens with anyone in any part of the world ... in my view, it is imperative that these populations should be taken into account, because, at this precise moment, even today, they still continue to be the target for violent attack or physical injury, imposed upon them by the western expansion still in progress and activated by both western foreigners and their own westernised compatriots ...

... I have not been given a mandate by anyone to come here and speak on behalf of anyone at all ... I speak for myself ... I do not defend any cause, I merely assume a question that relates to my own reason for existing ... but I cannot avoid stressing, whenever I am called upon to express my opinion about questions relating to the place of the Other, how distraught I am, to put it mildly, to see populations that were previously besieged by agents of westernisation imposing upon them the need to accept the signs and the ways of the western world and technological progress, and who are today still besieged by these same or similar agents now seeking to impose upon them the preservation of the signs and ways of their archaic and non-western models because this has insinuated itself as the most profitable both for some of them and for the Others provided that they allow themselves to be included on the menus of tourist programmes and allow themselves to be represented as expressions of an ecological and redeeming exoticness alongside other bizarre attractions such as herds of zebras, elephants and gazelles... .

... don't ask me what solutions I propose for problems of this nature ... I'm not a politician, or a prophet or a militant belonging to any movement whatsoever ... but you will certainly have the right to ask me where I am trying to get to if I don't have any proposals for saving the "Other", and yet even so I invite you to take this Other into consideration and to listen to him, even though I also do not propose that you should go there and listen to what the elders may have to teach you ... what type of action or attitude thus leads me to wish to hold your attention?

... what I propose is quite simple and within reach of those who are interested and professionals that can be brought together in relation to questions of this nature ... it is not a question of having a particular path to propose ... it is, instead, a question of having some ideas for the possibility of helping to discover a path ... accepting a possible disturbance, reconfiguration or even a prospective, pragmatic and programmatic replacement for the western/global/universal cosmogonic, cognitive, institutional and political paradigm, resorting to other paradigmatic frameworks ... it would not be a question of introducing any kind of makeshift remedy, compensation or arrangement in the fields of the humanist paradigm, but rather trying to configure, or reconfigure, a new paradigm ... under the scope of this proposal, the hypothesis would only be contemplated on the basis of the identification, convening and possible integration of data originating from other frameworks of conception, cognition, representation and action akin to African and other geneses ... it would certainly not be a question of trying to sustain change but of calling upon other forms of knowledge, other visions, other ways, other possibilities of change beyond the one that is imposed by the western programme ... it wouldn't even be a question of seeking to replace one paradigm with another or proposing one that is better than the other ... but only of suggesting some form of action that would be capable of extracting what is known, and drawing upon all means and expressions, finding some better way of dealing with all manner of obstacles, without always creating new civilisational obstacles and adding new obstacles to all manner of already existing ones...

... returning to my proposal: might it not be possible to envisage drawing upon paradigms other than that of western humanism and extracting from them something that genuinely satisfies the global interest, which has itself been indelibly marked and guided by the model that the West has imposed on the whole world and which still continues to expand?

... but then, if my programme does not involve listening willingly, folklorically and militantly to what the elders may have to teach us, what does it involve? It may perhaps, very orthodoxly and academically (and this will be my succinct, simple and discreet programme), involve looking at what western expansion itself has produced as a record about the "Other" ... a re-reading, and therefore a revisiting, of what has been written ... but not a classical and critical re-reading ... rather attempting to glean and extract what may lie behind the ethnographic documents that have been used, if these exist, or the texts that have been produced without their authors taking into account the possibility of there being any other paradigm that is worthy of some consideration ... a re-reading therefore that might attempt to discover another perspective, and in fact precisely a perspective that could take into account other ways for humankind to see its relationship with the rest of creation, that might therefore afford us both an importance and a pertinence that are different, from paradigms other than the western humanist paradigm that has imposed itself, taken control and therefore now reigns supreme ... that might even take into account the fact that this would perhaps be a genuinely innovative opportunity for the westernised intellectuals, *Others* and 'Others', that have emerged from the field both of the 'Other' and of the *Other*, and who are always called upon, without any alternative, to situate their affirmation and their performance in the terrains and arenas where the knowledge and power of the western matrix are exercised ... they might therefore finally intervene in a way that could save them from giving in to the folklore of authenticatory or renaissance fantasies and ethnic and tourist-based collaborationism and, after all, open up a path whereby we might also claim for ourselves the right to make demands ... I have long been saying that the prevailing scientific intellectuality will only really mean anything to us when it is forced to incorporate into global science something that comes from a matrix that is unequivocally our own ...

... the programme that I would therefore venture to suggest here, without exactly knowing who I should propose it to, would be to envisage an action that is based from the outset on making a general re-reading of everything that has been recorded about our knowledge of the Other, about the knowledge of Others, in the light of the possibility of admitting the existence and potential pertinence of other paradigms for assessing the relationship of people with the rest of creation, without also, from the outset, taking into account all the anti-humanist attacks that have been launched through the humanist paradigm itself in the course of its history and what in the meantime will be done, and is in fact being done at this very moment, in relation to the same objective, even though it may be formulated otherwise ...

... a programme, therefore, that could respond to our concerns, and go some way towards solving our problems and overcoming the obstacles of the present-day world, but which also aims far beyond the salvationist and do-good practices that we currently see in progress and which, after all, do not manage to call into question any system, however harmful it may have shown itself to be ... which instead aims to effect such an absolute turnaround in our way of looking at the world that this might constitute a quantum leap, a transformation, a bias that is capable of inspiring a framework for the relationship of man with the rest of creation and with the world in general that is very different from the one that the humanist programme has designed for the future of the world, to the point of its currently upsetting the present in such a way that everyone is running scared … which could point once again to different practices that might even end up suiting everybody, even those whose only wish is to take advantage of the fact that they control and dominate everything … a programme, in fact, that would at least create the possibility of authorising someone to experiment, to try, to see what it may perhaps be immediately possible to discover without making too much noise or spending too much money … which might just, perhaps (who knows?) make it possible to set some scholars to work studying and at least reviewing everything that has been established, gathered together and written about other cultures … new readings that might allow us to extract new ideas from the same materials … is there really nothing that was previously scorned and overlooked, but which can now be extracted from the animist paradigm, for example, in accordance with the new visions, new questions and new interests that are currently asserting themselves in this world? In this way, perhaps, the characters in the book that I have been writing might then find fertile ground for proposing their guardian hero, that Nambalisita, the ecological hero and kindred spirit, who is a man and a hero over and beyond the humanist condition and graced with a divine genealogy that so far has only been concerned with men of certain colours and a certain culture and has been giving them the legitimacy and the authority to control and regulate everything, the entire creation, including men of other colours …

… and perhaps I might then finally find justification for definitively formulating what I have been striving after and promising for so long: a neo-animist manifesto proposed to the entire world as one of the paths of such a pragmatic turnaround and leading to a paradigm shift capable of giving both a place and direction to all existences – divine, biological and even mineral …

Translated by John Elliott

An Intercultural Approach to the Issue of Islamic Extremism[*]

SHERIFA ZUHUR

Is it possible to apply an intercultural approach to the issue of Islamic extremism? *Can* we, divided as we are by national, ethnic and religious identities, or ideological or disciplinary frameworks? How do we create such an approach, given destructive and unpredictable extremist actions, and the destructive impact of western responses meant to defeat them? Is it possible to employ intercultural and cosmopolitan solutions, beyond introductory exchanges or presentations in which we only hint at the difficulties of pursuing cooperation that is more than multicultural or comparative. Many divisions have arisen in us, in part from the Global War on Terror and the so-called 'war of ideas' within it. Do we dare naively ignore the incentives that arms industries, contractors, departments of defence, security personnel – indeed, the entire 'terrorism industry' – have to prolong the 'long war'?

It is not clear that all parties believe there is a *need* for an intercultural approach. The American prescription for the Global War

* These views are not necessarily those of the US Department of Defense, or Department of the Army.

on Terror is not a feasible, or even distasteful but necessary option; it heightened the global conflict that fuels extremist recruitment. This situation is due to (a) flawed analyses of the appeal of bin Laden and al-Qa'ida – in the West, blaming the supposedly failed civilisation of Muslims[1] or their 'failed states'; (b) broadening the scope of America's enemies so that the war on terror targets many local nationalist struggles in addition to 'global jihad' and (c) wrong actions taken to carry out the Global War on Terror. Public opinion surveys in 2007 and 2008 in six Arab countries showed that people believed the threat of al-Qa'ida was exaggerated. In the 2008 Zogby-Telhami study, the two greatest threats to security were listed by survey respondents as Israel (95%) and the United States (88%), not Iran. Those surveyed believed that Iraqis were far worse off now than before, and that the highly touted surge strategy in Iraq had not decreased, or only temporarily decreased violence, which they fear may move into their own countries.[2]

In the West, the approach to the issues implicitly links Muslims and Islam with violence and anti-democratic thinking. Westerners constantly ask why Muslims or their leaders haven't repudiated violence or jihad; certainly I hear this comment on most occasions when I speak.[3] Muslims are asking different and extremely vital questions –why is the West waging war, or promoting enforced regime change or reform in their countries?

The most correct way to approach Islamic extremism, or Islamic terrorism, is to see it as a variant of extremism, and terrorist tactics in general. Yet, there is an ideological and not merely a psychological or individual aspect to recruitment and we see that extremists or insurgents and their governments and western governments hold conflicting visions of the public good and social justice.

A 'new jihad', which is far from being entirely new, has sparked hundreds of violent incidents, which some call a global *salafi* or global jihadist network. But that is certainly not all there is to the encounters and tensions between the West and the Muslim world. Far better armed is a globalised western network waging war on Muslim principles in the name of the war on terror that premises its endeavour on the supposed 'clash of civilisations'. When Muslims state, as they have in the previous years of the survey mentioned and many other surveys, that they feel or fear there is a war on Islam, we are hearing the effect of the war of ideas.

If Islamic extremism is an easily defined and addressed problem, then why haven't Muslim governments defeated it? What lessons shall we draw from the current and previous failures of counter-insurgency and counterterrorist doctrine? Various country cases show that Islamic movements can increase or decrease the tactical use of violence[4] and also that some level of volunteerist violence is uncontrolled by particular movements.[5] Governments claim to have vanquished movements through forceful counterterrorist measures, yet in some cases, these movements went underground, or into exile, becoming more vengeful and violent than previously.

Jihadist movements glorify a struggle, in which their deaths inspire new martyrs. Isn't that a good reason to look for intercultural input on ways to disassociate martyrdom from jihad? Are there different ways to discourage young people from wilfully pursuing death, and show that the patient, arduous pursuit of jihad in its non-violent form is infinitely more beneficial to the Muslim community?

When jihadist movements recanted the use of violence, as seen with the Muslim Brotherhood of Egypt, the Wasatiyya, and after 1999, with the Jama`at Islamiyya and Jihad Islami, the leadership was acting pragmatically. This meant different things – for the Muslim Brotherhood it meant preservation of their movement and acceptance of its status as a socio-religious movement and not a legal political party. For Hamas and Hizbullah, change meant participating in the political process and reining in violence (although not respectively relinquishing the national struggle, and the protection of Lebanese territory against Israel). In the more radical Egyptian Jihad Islami and Jama`at Islamiyya, arch-jihadists disseminated arguments against violent jihad[6] from prison thereby adding to a Muslim discourse of anti-terrorism (some of these principles are now operative in the Saudi anti-terrorist, or violence reduction campaign,[7] although the relationship of the ideas might not be admitted).

This suggests that a truly intercultural approach would not iterate universalist or preemptive doctrines, but rather consider the problems of Islamic extremism in their specific context.

The contemporary discussion of cosmopolitanism concerns the benefits of different world views and priorities. If the cosmopolitan is a citizen of the world, or one who ruefully or joyfully accepts multiple identities, her or his transglobal perspective should matter. So too should those of non-western communities, non-state or civil society actors as well as non-western governments.

I would suggest that to be effective, an intercultural approach should focus on the narrower issue of the violence involved in Islamic extremism rather than attempt broader deradicalisation which requires more symmetry or replication of values. Red lines, like an absolute end to torture, violence, attacks on citizens and abuse of justice, could be imposed. And that means limiting state terrorism as well as non-state terrorism.

A religious awakening or revival has affected the Muslim world since the early 1970s. The tensions between western economic, cultural and political dominance, and the western secularist model greatly complicate views of this awakening (*sahwa* in Arabic) and various resultant Muslim debates. One debate has concerned the role of the state and its alliances with the West; others revolve around the proper status of an Islamic society, of laws, of freedom of expression, women's rights, and development.

Approaches now iterated in the West are imprecise and illogical and rely on conquest, binarism and theologocentrism. These approaches are imprecise first because they falsely or selectively describe aspects of Islamic thought and belief to impute totalitarian tendencies while removing liberties in the name of security. Secondly, the war of ideas misidentifies the Enemy – lumping together violent and non-violent 'radicals' or extremists, together with ordinary Muslims. Thirdly, it promises too much – to address real and potential threats in Muslim communities everywhere in the world. Fourthly, it engages in *takfir*, or binarism, in asserting the ability to separate the good Islam from the bad. This is truly a mimicking of the extremists' charge that their rulers are so opposed to the Muslim ethic that they are not Muslims.

The war of ideas blurs the eclectic and variant nature of Islamic institutions and concepts, and resurrects neocolonialism in promoting moderate westernised identities for Muslims, who should perforce discard their traditional, medieval views.

The whole project is troubled by theologocentrism[8] and neo-Orientalism. Focusing entirely on the faith dimension of Muslim society, and disregarding the Muslim as a social or political or economic actor, greatly complicates intercultural understanding. For example, at least half of the most radical Egyptian groups' stated grievances, like al-Qa'ida's, are political in nature. Theologocentrism makes it more difficult to interpret social data. Socially learned standards mean that Muslim citizens may not report changing indicators of religiosity if they imply previous disregard for religious requirements. Or women may not report men's alcoholism or drug abuse in evaluations of men's violence against women, which both men and women wrongly believe to be a prerogative of Muslim men, like polygyny.[9] Also consider how experts highlight exotic aspects of Muslim practice to imply retrogression, or lack of rationality, as when Shi'i millenarian beliefs about the coming of the Imam Mahdi are cited in discussions about Iranian nuclear development.[10]

Orientalism furthered a political project of domination.[11] The Global War on Terror expresses a neo-Orientalism, as recently illustrated in a hideous DVD entitled *Obsession*. It was distributed by 22 American newspapers, including the *Chronicle of Higher Education*, funded by the mysterious Clarion Foundation, most probably in an attempt to aid 2008 US presidential candidate John McCain at the polls.

On the other side of the world, one notes an extreme paranoia of western attacks on the region or specific countries. Some Muslim groups attribute these attacks to Christian religious zeal or a new Crusade, which is probably a misanalysis. Also, we see the emergence of a new *fiqh* (jurisprudence) of jihad – asserted by extremists – which ignores many of the important limitations that operate as checks and balances in the classical tradition.

The American government confuses international cooperation with an intercultural approach to the war on terror, citing the multinational force in Iraq (overwhelmingly subject to US direction), ongoing military coordination with counterparts, like joint exercises and visits, and some international meetings dealing with counterterrorism. In these, only the western paradigms of counter-insurgency theory matter, and the 'metrics of success' concern the degree to which other sovereign nations enact the policies that the US promotes – democratisation, anti-corruption, now entitled 'rule of law', or reform, attacking non-state actors engaged in violence, and acceptance of the counterterrorist policies of strike or clear, hold and build – meaning that force, not diplomacy, is the primary element of power utilised.

The former President George W. Bush referred to Islamic terrorists' aim to create a caliphate as the terrifying end-state desired by America's enemies. His neoconservative supporters (and others) attacked basic Islamic concepts – like the *ummah* (the community of Muslims believers), the caliphate, the *shari'ah* and *tawhid*.[12] I confess to being particularly shocked by Davies's study which proposed various ways of countering Muslim attempts to identify with their *ummah* or *shari'ah*. In addition, Muslim chari-ties, zakat committees and Islamic education and discourse in general were all under fire. Virtually all Muslim charities in the USA were attacked, or closed, many for supposed connections to Islamist organisations. Schools and charities have been attacked, indicted and closed, as in the West Bank in the summer of 2008 and turned over to Fatah because that party is deemed more secu-larist. Many have decried Muslims' ability to be democratic, particularly if they are Islamists, and take issue with Muslim women's dress, and with Muslims' reverence for their Prophet, their holy book and observance of basic faith features. Vast sums are being spent to force, convince or teach Muslim preachers to express more moderate views. Some aspects of these efforts alienate Muslims who were to date our allies, and will not convince any committed to long-term resistance.

The Caliphate

The caliphate became a new Evil Empire in the American discourse on the Global War on Terror. It was a political institution that defined the head of state after the Prophet's death. At first selected by a group of community leaders, the caliphate became a troubled hereditary office under the Ummayyad rulers, and eventually a sort of endorsing presence for the Mamluks,[13] although the caliph was a virtual prisoner of his sultan. A caliphate or imamate was considered more ideal than a tribal or monarchic system, because the caliph would uphold the shari`ah, Islamic law, thus ensuring justice and not tyranny. It is wrong to denigrate this historic – yet highly impractical – ideal for ordinary Muslims. It has an important place in the intercultural discussion of government. Yet Muslims, so deeply divided by local histories and postcolonial national identities, are not likely to reunite in the political form of the *ummah*, the caliphate (rather it is a reference point for potential cooperation and identification of shared interests) – unless they are attacked and goaded into doing so in a global war. Attacking this aspect of Muslim heritage is as wrong as it is to claim that Muslims oppose democracy.

Democracy

The Qur'ān does not specify the caliphate. Still, it was a revered concept and suggestions that it was *not* the ideal system provided the basis of the controversial trial of 'Ali abd al-Raziq, an early twentieth-century Egyptian thinker.[14] Therefore, quite a few other thinkers, including Islamists, have argued that a democratic Islamic state could arise, or one in which executive powers were more balanced with others than at present. Islamists supporting democracy naturally emphasise an Islamic state with a democratic method rather than a democratic state of Muslims with no Islamic identity or legal system. Indeed, Abd al-Karim Soroush, an Iranian scholar, states that because Islam supports and requires freedom, it is a necessary complement to democracy.[15] On the other hand, the al-Qa'ida rejoinder is that a democracy that represents the will of the majority and not the sovereignty of God is not Islamically permitted, and al-Qa'ida has complained of other Islamist groups' (Hamas, Hizbullah) participation in political processes not strictly

Islamic. Not only al-Qa'ida argues against democracy, other Muslim thinkers do so because the aim of western-style democracy (the currently accepted meaning) would not necessarily support Islamic law, morality or social justice.

Sectarianism and Democracy

However, implanting US or Italian or any other form of western, or even non-western, democracy, in the region may heighten sectarianism, political and ethnic conflict, until new methods of power sharing are devised. In Friday sermons across Iraq, the US Senate's proposal[16] to federalise and partition Iraq was criticised. Shaykh Abd al-Mahdi al-Karbala'i, a spokesman for Grand Ayatollah `Ali Sistan, said: 'The division plan is against Iraq's interests and against peace in a united Iraq.'[17] That sectarianism is an evil that divides Muslims was echoed in the mosques under Ayatollah Sistani's authority. We hear a similar theme in King Abdullah of Saudi Arabia's speeches concerning *fitna*, schism between Muslims, which is a major, negative outcome of western policies in the Middle East and the tactics adopted in inter-Muslim tensions. (Sectarianism's evils were painfully evident in civil war Lebanon,[18] and re-emerged following the so-called Cedar Revolution.)

Many Muslim governments have long suppressed or stifled their political oppositions. Parties struggling against them say that efforts to promote democracy 'must engage Islam' and that political reform will fail if Islamists are excluded.[19] The West is calling for secularist democracy, and for the protection of individual rights and freedoms that have not been a part of public life everywhere in the world. Certain individual rights appear to Muslims to collide with their collectivist definition of Islamic duties.[20]

Moderates

Westerners allude to a civil war in Islam, between 'orthodox and reformers'.[21] Analysts at the Rand Corporation claim that existing

Muslim moderates are not sufficiently moderate at all and cannot participate in the transformative process needed to bolster 'moderate Muslim values' because they have not assimilated in Europe (and the USA) and don't accept secularism.[22] Expectations that Muslims should make religion private, and embrace western cultural values, not condemn Israel, or not support Palestinians, not follow Islamic law, or enthusiastically back American foreign policy are unreasonable.

A different definition of 'moderation' is being promoted in Saudi Arabia, Jordan and Yemen. It is intended to diminish *takfiri*st orientations, and to dispel critiques of governments being insufficiently Islamic. Here, the intent is to modify the zeal for the *hisba*, or the command to install what is lawful and reject what is evil. Allusions are made to the recommendations toward moderation uttered by the Prophet Muhammad (*s.a.w.s.*) himself, who understood that extreme strictness or rigour would discourage believers from his path.

Preachers and Clerics

Great misunderstandings circulate around Islamic thought and the role of Islamic scholars, educators and preachers, who supposedly have not condemned 9/11, when indeed they have condemned this attack, or more generally, violent attacks on innocents (with the exclusion of Muslims facing occupation as in Palestine; however, some have even condemned such attacks under any circumstances).[23] One intent of the Global War on Terror is to contain 'radical messages' by clerics, while some wanted Muslims to seize this moment of critique to reform or undo the `ulama's (the clerics') hold on religious authority.[24]

It is often misunderstood that the clerical establishment is not monolithic,[25] nor anti-modern[26] and is in somewhat of a state of crisis, after being affected by more than a century of erosion and containment by the governments of modern nation states.[27] Another difficult notion to grasp is that the very separation between the religious and political sphere that westerners want

Muslims to experience has long been protected in a very important way by the religious leaders' ability to speak out against
unlawful governments or politics from a protected religious
space.[28]

Western Global War on Terror recommendations include
book-banning, requiring new teachings and terms for jihad
(*'munfasid'* [evil-doer], argues Jim Girard of Truth Speak, while
'murji'' [with the meaning of retrograde] is a problematic term
suggested by some Muslims eager to decry bin Ladin; contrast with
'insane evil-doers' as the code word for violent extremists in Egypt)
and enforced muzzling, firing or reforming of preachers. Given a
policy whereby nations like Saudi Arabia were blamed for the intellectual climate leading to al-Qa'ida, quite a bit of pressure to reform
these sectors has been brought to bear.

As explained above, political protest expressed in religious
spaces has sometimes provided the only counter to and haven
from despotism. The independence of religious messages and
spaces are exceedingly important in Muslim communities, so feelings are mixed about governmental and western oversight in the
retraining of preachers intended to limit their freedom of expression. 'Establishment Islam' is not always viewed positively, so the
consequences of this new tactic could further fission the fabric of
Muslim discourse.

Qur'ān

Strongly worded attacks on parts of the Qur'ān, especially those
sections known as the Sword Verses, are now a staple of counterterrorist doctrine in the West, often accompanied by strong
criticism of Wahhabism, or Saudi orthodoxy. Here, westerners see
a link to the *'ulama'*s support for the legitimacy of defensive or
collectively required *jihad*,[29] but the Qur'ān's historicity and acces-
sibility to Muslims is misunderstood by novice readers. The Qur'ān
becomes a symbol for Islamophobia, denigrated at Guantanamo,
and shot at in Iraq. It is in Qur'ānic and Islamic legal principles that
we can find some important justifications for the defusing of

violence and possible common ground between rulers/governments and public opposition such as *maslaha* (the common or public good)[30] and `*adalah* (social justice).

Secularism

The war of ideas' rigid insistence on 'secular Islam' is somewhat at odds with the ascendance of the religious Right's platform in the Republican party in the USA. For their part, Muslims have often misunderstood secularism to be a system that counters religion,[31] (and similarly oppose socialism and communism). One cannot be identified as a secular Muslim in much of the Islamic world, only a 'liberal' or a 'modern' one, and Fauzi Najjar notes, 'Muslims have found it more convenient to circumvent, rather than to change, the [Islamic] law.'[32]

Coercing elites or governments in the Muslim world to secularise or promote secularism is one issue, but living as Muslims in a 'secular' western society is another matter. Unfortunately, much of the war on terror thinking encompasses other problems that are seen in the absorption of Muslim immigrants in the West. We often invoke ideas about the world's 'globalisation' (economic), yet as a well-known Islamist spokesman, Selim al-Awa notes, all the terms of today's globalised world are really western.[33] That means that Muslim currents in globalisation, like other eastern ones, are ignored.

Certain Muslims do prioritise their needs as believers, and try to retain their cultural, religious, social and political identities in secular Europe and the less secular USA,[34] a fact protested by many in Europe. One issue is their adherence to Islamic law, and the conflicts that may arise with local laws due to their social practice, and dealing with racism and anti-terrorist attitudes and policies.

Islamist Ali Kettani of Morocco recommended that Muslims maintain their own enclaves in the West, thus retaining control over their own and their children's identities.[35] This way of organising social life is more easily accomplished in areas with a denser immigrant population, and is more difficult elsewhere. It parallels activities by Jewish and Christian communities, hence, one may argue that deradicalisation cannot be accomplished by denying a cohesive identity (whether one likes the way it is emerging or not) to some groups but not others. Even when (American) Muslims are not in any type of 'radical' atmosphere, it has been shown that they are more aware of, and amenable to, civic practices, for instance in obtaining aid or solving problems, when they are part of mosque communities.[36] That is, religious organisation can provide a sense of how to better live in and negotiate a secular and foreign environment.

In addition, the war on ideas indicts basic terms of Islamic identity and unity so that Muslims who refer to the need for Muslim unity, or their belief in absolute monotheism or unicity (*tawhid*, what Fazlur Rahman called the 'master-truth' of the Qur'ān[37]) and other doctrines may be deemed extremists. This is very problematic – there are good reasons that intercultural approaches would stress Muslim unity. It is exceedingly fragile, and so many political and security situations are compromised due to severe factionalism.

There is no scope in this paper to present the obstacles to interculturality that exist in the Muslim world, but they certainly exist, are multiplying and are worth exploring. Intercultural relations are skewed in Muslim nations where numerous refugees and contract workers experience exploitation and racism, and public policy solutions have been ineffective.

Women

In the war of ideas, Muslim women are addressed as a key constituency for democratisation of the region, whereas Islam is construed as the force that prevents women (and all of society) from achieving their potential. Those seeking to create 'new Muslim moderates' are banking on women's support to end harmful practices.[38]

As a woman, I am aware of the unequal status of women in the Muslim world who face statutory discrimination,[39] honour crimes,[40] severe cultural pressure and, usually, little support from religious authorities. So one cannot help noticing that the impact of the Global War on Terror and the shock of additional attacks from Iraq to Amman to Casablanca have been helpful to certain reforms for women, while structural disadvantages and cultural impediments remain. When heads of state back reform issues, as in Egypt in the newly reformed child's rights law, or in Morocco new approaches to family law (the *mudawana*), the additional factor of the post-9/11 environment has worked in their favour. A strong backlash is occurring, as activists on the other side learned they could enforce cancellation of segments of reforms – as with the women's right to travel in the 2000 family law reform in Egypt.[41] Women have benefited, both from the imposition of universalist scrutiny, and from intercultural approaches, although their aims can be subordinated to struggles over political power. In Iraq, modernist family law legislation of the 1960s[42] is now swept away and an uneasy coexistence of civil law and shariah replaces it. Over these war-filled years, extremists targeted women business owners and drivers, no matter how they were dressed.[43] Legal reform progressed in the Kurdish areas, but tragic self-immolations of girls and young women continue there. Recently, women in Iran demonstrated against a new law that the Iranian parliament was considering which would do away with notice to the first wife in cases of polygamy. It seems logical to ask that reforms that address violence or extreme harm to women be the first priority of reform, but it is not so easy to overcome popular understandings of Islamic law and cultural practice. This brief discussion is not a digression from the main issue, but rather evidence that 'terror' is only constructed as Islamic attacks on the West, and not all forms of violence, even including the myriad forms unleashed on women.

To conclude, an intercultural approach would relinquish the term 'Islamofascism' and instead of Islamofascism Week (as now introduced on American college campuses annually by Horowitz et al.), institute an Intercultural Solutions Week – an endeavour to establish a real exchange of ideas with Muslims (and not only with their governments) in the struggle against terrorism, as well as in cooperative efforts to aid social change and development.

An intercultural approach to Islamic extremism must engage with foreign policies that have detrimental effects on Muslim populations. It must come to terms with the admiration for bin Laden in the region, without denying its existence. It must not preface the establishment of a global security service or Global Homeland/Lands Security that patrols the world, confusing insurgent and terrorist threats. It must not preclude life with the Other.

Notes

1 Here I agree with Michael Scheuer, *Imperial Hubris: Why the West is Losing the War on Terror* (Washington, DC: Potomac Books, 2004), pp. 109–115, although I have arrived at my conclusions on a different route and, unlike Mr Scheuer, I do not believe the USA should eschew international cooperation, retreat and close its borders, and deny human rights issues, such as the Darfur or Gazan crises. Scheur, unpublished evening lecture, Carr Center, Dickinson College, Carlisle, PA, 12 February 2009.

2 Anwar Sadat Chair for Peace and Development, University of Maryland, with Zogby International, '2008 Annual Arab Public Opinion Poll', March 2008.

3 For example, Thomas Friedman wrote, 'To this day – to this day – no major Muslim cleric or religious body has ever issued a fatwa condemning Osama bin Laden', *New York Times*, 8 July 2005. This is false. One problem is the paucity of US media references to clerics' statements, gatherings and websites (unless they are violent declarations). For instance, this fatwa announced at the 2008 Hyderabad conference: 'Islam rejects all kinds of unjust violence, breach of peace, bloodshed, murder and plunder and does not allow it in any form. Cooperation should be done for the cause of good but not for committing sin or oppression', which was produced by the Darul Ulum Deoband, India's premier Islamic seminary. Accessed at http://www.upi.com, 8 November 2008. Spanish Muslim clerics issued a fatwa against bin Laden: http://www.csmonitor.com/2005/0314/p06s01-woeu.html. Many other statements have been gathered by Alan Godlas at the University of Georgia on this resource page http://www.uga.edu/islam/.

4 Quintan Wiktorowicz (ed.), *Islamic Activism: A Social Movement Theory*

Approach (Bloomington, IN: Indiana University Press, 2004).

5 John Burns, 'Osama Stirs Struggle on Meaning of Jihad', *New York Times*, 27 January 2002. http://www.sullivan-county.com/identity/bin_laden.html

6 Sharifa Zuhur, 'Motivational Known and Unknown Aspects of Radicalisation and Deradicalisation in the New Jihad in Saudi Arabia and Beyond', in T. Pick and A. Speckhardt (eds), *Radicalisation and Deradicalisation in Immigrant Communities and their Countries of Origin*, forthcoming; Salwa El Awa, *The Militant Islamic Group in Egypt 1974–2006 [Al-Jama'a Al-Islamiyya al-Musallaha fi Misr 1974–2006]* (Cairo: Maktabat al-Shuruq al-Duwaliyya, 2006).

7 Zuhur, 'Motivational Known and Unknown Aspects' and Zuhur, *Decreasing Violence in Saudi Arabia and Beyond* (University of Birmingham, forthcoming 2009).

8 Maxime Rodinson, *La Fascination de l'Islam* (Paris: La Decouverte, 1989); As'ad AbuKhalil, *Bin Laden, Islam and America's New 'War on Terrorism'* (New York: Seven Stories, 2002).

9 Essam Fawzy, 'Muslim Personal Status Law in Egypt: The Current Situation and Possibilities of Reform through Internal Initiatives', in Lynn Welchman (ed.), *Women's Rights and Islamic Family Law* (London: Zed Books, 2004).

10 Sherifa Zuhur, *Iraq, Iran, and the United States: The New Triangle's Impact on Sectarianism and the Nuclear Threat* (Carlisle: Strategic Studies Institute, 2006).

11 Edward Said, *Orientalism* (New York: Vintage Books, 1978); Edmond Burke and David Prochaska (eds), *Genealogies of Orientalism: History, Theory, Politics* (Lincoln, NE: University of Nebraska Press, 2008).

12 Jacquelyn Davis (principal investigator) and IFPA, *Radical Islamic Ideologies and Implications for US Strategic Planning and US Central Command's Operations* (Cambridge, MA: Institute for Foreign Policy Analysis, January 2007); also Michael Doran, 'The Saudi Paradox', *Foreign Affairs*, January/February, 2004.

13 Thomas W. Arnold, *The Caliphate* (Oxford: Clarendon Press, 1924).

14 Sherifa Zuhur, *Precision in the Global War on Terror: Inciting Muslims through the War of Ideas* (Carlisle: Strategic Studies Institute, 2008), pp. 24–25; Leonard Binder, *Islamic Liberalism: A Critique of Development Ideologies* (Chicago: University of Chicago Press, 1988), pp. 128–69, esp. p. 131).

15 'Islam and democracy are not only compatible, their association is inevitable. In a Muslim society, one without the other is not perfect.'

Soroush as quoted from interviews in Tehran and Washington, DC, in 1994 and 1995. Robin Wright, 'Islam and Liberal Democracy: Two Visions of Reformation', *Journal of Democracy* 7.2, 1996, pp. 64–75.

16 Joseph R. Biden and Leslie H. Gelb, 'Unity Through Autonomy in Iraq', *New York Times*, 6 May 2006, http://query.nytimes.com/gst/fullpage.html?res+9405EEDE113FF932A35756C0A9609C8B63. Joseph Biden is now US vice-president and Gelb was president emeritus of the Council on Foreign Relations. Biden insisted during the presidential campaign that the plan was not a 'partition' but it was difficult for Iraqis to perceive it any other way. The plan did not address the issue of the mixed (Sunni and Shi'a) centre of Iraq.

17 *Washington Post*, 28 September 2007.

18 Martin Kramer, 'The Oracle of Hizbullah: Sayyid Muhammad Husayn Fadlallah', Part 2. http://www.geocities.com/martinkramerorg/Oracle2.htm#n124.

19 'Democratizing the Middle East?' Fares Center for Eastern Mediterranean Studies, Occasional Paper No. 2, 2006. A report on the conference, 'Democratizing the Middle East?', held January 26–27, 2006, p. 5.

20 For a lengthier discussion, see Zuhur, *Precision in the Global War on Terror*.

21 Davis and IFPA, *Radical Islamic Ideologies*, p. 4.

22 Angel Rabasa, Cheryl Bernard, Lowell H. Schwartz and Peter Sickle, *Building Moderate Muslim Networks* (Santa Monica, CA: RAND Corporation, 2007).

23 Diyala Hamzah, 'Is There an Arab Public Sphere? The Palestinian Intifada, a Saudi Fatwa and the Egyptian Press', in Armando Salvatore and Mark Levine (eds), *Religion, Social Practice and Contested Hegemonies: Reconstructing the Public Sphere in Muslim Majority Societies* (New York: Palgrave MacMillan, 2005); also Zuhur, *Precision in the Global War on Terror*.

24 This idea has been suggested by Muslim thinkers as well. With regard to rethinking the status of women in Islam, this is probably an important endeavour. See Khaled Abou El Fadl, *Speaking in God's Name: Islamic Law, Authority, and Women* (Oxford: Oneworld Publications, 2001).

25 Lindsay Wise, 'Amr Khaled vs. Yusuf Al Qaradawi: The Danish Cartoon Controversy and the Clash of Two Islamic TV Titans', *TBS* 16, 2006, http://www.tbsjournal.com/Wise.htm.

26 Richard Antoun, *Muslim Preacher in the Modern World: A Jordanian Case*

Study (Princeton, NJ: Princeton University Press, 1989); Patrick Gaffney, *The Prophet's Pulpit: Islamic Preaching in Contemporary Egypt* (Berkeley, CA: University of California Press, 1994); Nashwa Abdel-Tawab, 'TV Preachers in Egypt: Religion Anyone?' *Al-Ahram Weekly*, Issue 765, 20–26 October 2005.

27 Noah Feldman, *The Fall and Rise of the Islamic State* (Princeton, NJ: Princeton University Press, 2008).

28 See Bast and Haram in Zuhur, *Precision in the Global War on Terror*, pp. 28–29; 54–55; see also Patrick Haenni and Husam Tammam, 'Egypt's Air-Conditioned Islam', *Le Monde Diplomatique*, September 2003.

29 Hamzah, 'Is There an Arab Public Sphere?'

30 Muhammad Q. Zaman, 'The `Ulama of Contemporary Islam and their Conceptions of the Common Good', in Armando Salvatore and Dale Eickelman (eds), *Public Islam and the Common Good* (Leiden: Brill, 2004).

31 S. Abid Husain, *The Destiny of Indian Muslims* (New York: Asia Publishing House, 1965), p. 170.

32 Fauzi Najjar, 'The Arabs, Islam, and Globalization', *Middle East Policy* 12.3, Fall 2005, p. 94.

33 `Awwa in Najjar, 'The Arabs, Islam and Globalization', pp. 94–95.

34 Olivier Roy, *Secularism Confronts Islam*, trans. George Holoch (New York: Columbia University Press, 2007).

35 M.A. Kettani, *Muslim Minorities in the World Today* (London: Mansell, 1986); see also Yvonne Haddad and John Esposito, 'The Dynamics of Islamic Identity in North America', in Haddad and Esposito, *Muslims on the Americanization Path* (New York: Oxford University Press, 2000), p. 8.

36 Amaney Jamal, 'The Political Participation and Engagement of Muslim Americans: Mosque Involvement and Group Consciousness', *American Politics Research* 33.4, 2005, pp. 521–44.

37 Fazlur Rahman, *Major Themes of the Qur'an* (Minneapolis: Bibliotheca Islamica, 1980); and for the opposite argument in which unicity is framed as totalitarian uniformity see Doran, 'The Saudi Paradox'.

38 Rabasa et al., *Building Moderate Muslim Networks*, p. 143.

39 Sherifa Zuhur, *Gender, Sexuality, and Criminal Laws in the Middle East and the Islamic World* (Istanbul: WWHR/New Ways, 2005).

40 Lamia Abu Odeh, 'Crimes of Honour and the Construction of Gender in Arab Societies', in Mai Yamani (ed.), *Feminism and Islam: Legal and Literary Perspectives* (Reading, UK: Ithaca Press and Centre for Islamic and Middle Eastern Law, University of London, 1996).

41 Sherifa Zuhur, 'The Mixed Impact of Feminist Struggles in Egypt During the 1990s', *Middle East Review of International Affairs* 5.1, March 2001.

42 See Fatima al-Hayani, 'Legal Modernism in Iraq: A Study of the Amendments to Family Law'. PhD dissertation, Department of Near Eastern Studies, University of Michigan, Ann Arbor, MI, 1993.

43 Sherifa Zuhur, *Iraq, Women's Empowerment, and Public Policy* (Carlisle: Strategic Studies Institute, 2007).

Closing Session
Can There Be Life Without the Other?
The Possibilities and Limits of
Interculturality

JORGE SAMPAIO

It was with the greatest pleasure that I was able to accept the kind invitation addressed to me by the President of the Calouste Gulbenkian Foundation and my dear friend, Dr Rui Vilar, to bring the work of this conference to an end. And doubly so, not just because of the theme that has been debated here, but also because of the remarkable opportunity that is offered by this initiative, which forms part both of the European Year of Intercultural Dialogue and of the extremely full programme that the Gulbenkian Foundation has drawn up around the problematics of migrations. One should further add to this set of reasons the particular significance that this conference has for the United Nations High Representative for the Alliance of Civilisations, not only because of the quality of the reflections that have been made here, and which are a valuable indicator of the complexity and difficulties involved in this task, but also because of the occasion that it has offered me to share some of my concerns with you. For all of these reasons, I wish to express my heartfelt thanks and congratulations to the Gulbenkian Foundation and to all those who have taken part in this conference for these two intense days of learning and reflection.

In fact, if there remained any doubts as to the meaning of the answer to the question that has brought us together here today – 'Can there be life without the Other?' – these two days of dialogue have clearly shown that we neither can nor wish to live without the others – please allow me to use the *plural* here – and that we are, in fact, condemned to live with one another.

My dear friends, I confess that what I have heard here, both yesterday and today, has not left me feeling unmoved – so that, this morning, I decided to alter the notes that I had originally prepared for this brief speech of mine.

It is always extremely rewarding to compare the knowledge that we have with that of others, to create overlaps in our different perspectives and to arrive at new prisms of analysis. Not least because of the position that I hold, I am greatly interested in the miscegenation of knowledge, approaches and experiences. I am interested in passing from the particular to the general and then returning from the general to the particular. I am interested in transversal concepts that allow me to design a solid strategy for action. For all of these reasons, please allow me to stress how important it is that the specialists, academics and researchers should make an effort to communicate and that they should devote more time to what is referred to today as 'public diplomacy' and which previously went by the name of 'the popularisation of knowledge' – or, in other words, what is important is for us to socialise academic knowledge, to enable democracy to benefit from science, and to ensure that there are more communicating vessels between the world that tends to close itself off from academic circles and society in general, including here the group of decision makers with their own responsibilities in the governance of public property. The complexity of the questions that we are faced with today calls for this kind of interchange, without which no vision of the future can be sustainable. This is the first appeal that I make to you today.

I further confess that conferences of this kind are also an exercise in patience and the recognition of ignorance, because we cannot claim that we are sufficiently well endowed from the intellectual point of view to understand the ins and outs of everything that we hear, the subtlety of some distinctions or even the full scope of certain statements that have been made. How often are we overcome with the impression that we behave like intruders in a conversation that we were not invited to take part in? How often do we feel that the language used is completely opaque, to the point of its appearing like a hermetic subcode, accessible only to a small group of specially initiated people?

And yet, there are always an infinite number of clues that are laid bare, a comment that remains in our mind, a new piece of information that we have learned, a reference that catches our attention, raising doubts and questions that we take home with us … and this is good, it is something that is highly positive and it is because of this that the exercise is so worthwhile!

The theme that has been discussed here – about the singular and the multiple, being and time, the self and the Other, essence and existence, individuation and socialisation, otherness and intersubjectivity, *homo sapiens*, the human being or person and our life in society – can be found running through the whole history of humanity. It has passed through philosophical reflection from mythical thought to the more recent theories of the logical limits of reason, it has fascinated poets and stimulated writers and, of course, it has given rise to a whole host of academic disciplines, ranging from sociology to psychology, but also including anthropology, ethnology, architecture and town planning, given the wide range of currents of thought and the multidisciplinarities that are possible.

Of course, this is not the path that I will choose to follow in entering into this discussion – I do not have sufficient knowledge, nor am I in any way qualified to speak upon the subject. Instead, I should like to try the reverse exercise of re-asking, in relation to everyday life, some of the questions that have been invoked at this conference. For, after all, what have we been talking about for these last two days? In what way does the question that served as the guiding thread – 'Can there be life without the Other?' – call upon us to act as individuals and citizens? In what way has this question become an absolutely central theme of our society? In what way has this theme of society also been transformed into a matter of foreign policy, into a priority of the international agenda and into one of the critical issues of world governance?

These, my friends, are the questions that I wish to develop here briefly. Please forgive me for returning in this way to the basics, to the fragmented and complex world of day-to-day life. And, to be even more concrete, I invite you to undertake a small exercise with me.

Let us take a closer look at some of the headlines that made the front pages in August and which, if the truth be told, had a little bit of the 'silly season' about them...

'American-Islamic group seeks title change for the forthcoming movie *Towelhead*, Reuters reported, because the term is considered a 'racial and religious slur'

'Muslim headscarves test the limits of German Tolerance' (Spiegel Online)

'Polémique sur Aïcha, la Mère des Croyants à propos d'un nouveau roman qui va paraître bientôt' (*Le Monde*)

'Les traductions vers l'arabe de Pinocchio et Harry Potter interdites en Israel' (*Le Monde*)

'Violence in India is fuelled by religious and economic divide' (*New York Times*)

'Thailand's smile fades – in recent weeks the border between northern Malaysia and southern Thailand has seen an increase in inter-religious violence' (BBC)

'Civilian casualties are mounting in the southern Philippines, where fighting between Muslim guerrillas and the army has killed up to 187 people in the past 10 days', Reuters reported.

'Anti-Semitism on rise in Europe – attacks against Jews in Europe have sharply increased, says a report by a European anti-racism watchdog'

'Far-right mobilizes against Cologne Mega-Mosque' (Spiegel Online)

'Integrating Islam into the West – for all its good intentions, European multiculturalism fails to make a place for religion' (Spiegel Online)

'Italy's fingerprinting of members of the country's Roma community is a direct act of racial discrimination, the European Parliament has said'

'Saudis launch Islamic unity drive – Saudi Arabia's monarch has urged Muslims to speak with one voice in preparation for inter-faith dialogue with the Jewish and Christian worlds'

'Tibet's spiritual leader has repeated his call for dialogue between Chinese and Tibetan leaders'

What am I seeking to suggest with these examples? Precisely to show how much the question of the Others, the question of how we can all live together, is today a burning social and political issue that challenges the very mechanisms of democracy, as well as world peace and stability.

Obviously, there have always been movements of populations. But today, mobility and migratory flows have become a constant feature of our lives, leading to a considerable increase in the density of the ethnic, cultural and religious fabric of most of our societies. In Europe, this is a particularly visible reality, with Portugal, in fact, being an emblematic case, through its having also become transformed into a country of immigration, sought after by people that one would never have imagined would choose this to be their place of residence.

With regard to this particular issue, I always tend to remember a visit that I paid, when I was the Portuguese President, to a school in the periphery of Lisbon, where teachers had to deal with children of more than twenty different nationalities in the same class. Now I ask: in this concrete case, were the teachers trained to be able to make the most of such a diverse audience? Were they sufficiently prepared to act and react appropriately in this radically new situation? Had the school made adjustments to its everyday practices to be able to deal with this unusual reality of cultural and religious diversity in the community that it served?

Have the local parish and municipal councils devised a strategy of dialogue and integration in relation to the populations to which they play host? Are our cities – the quintessential place for the convergence and divergence of cultures, civilisations, histories and continents – prepared to deal with this new reality, to understand it and manage it appropriately? Have the public authorities developed a new concept of inclusive citizenship, dictated by a respect for fundamental rights and freedoms, equal opportunities and new practices of civic participation?

My friends, the Alliance of Civilizations, an initiative launched in 2005 (originally promoted by Spain and Turkey, but immediately endorsed by the United Nations), has precisely as its central objective to respond to this series of challenges. Our basic premise is that, if we do nothing – in political terms, not only at the global level, but also nationally and locally – the problems with which we are confronted today will degenerate into a conflict between cultures or, even worse, into a 'clash of civilisations'. And why are we so certain of this? Because of a whole host of signs and reasons, most notably: because we are faced with a global challenge, one that is common to all societies. Because we are forced to deal with a deep-rooted problem, which calls for long-term solutions, consisting essentially of preventive measures. Because, nowadays, a localised conflict can easily spread and, all of a sudden, become converted into a global crisis. Because all societies are confronted with extremism, radicalisation, an increase in violence, xenophobia and racism. Because the public authorities are experiencing a certain disorientation and impotence, due to the absence of suitable political instruments for intervening in an effective fashion. Because, after all, moderniszation, which we all thought would lead to a widespread secularisation of societies, has in fact increased the urgency of dealing with the religious question and sorting out the relationship between Church and State, between politics and religion, between temporal and spiritual power.

As far as I am concerned, I have no doubt that, at least in Europe, we are faced with an extensive challenge in deciding how best to integrate minorities, most particularly the Muslim minorities, and that this will only be achieved with a suitable policy, centred around the concept of an inclusive and participative citizenship, based on equal opportunities and a respect for cultural diversity. Similarly, I have no doubt that it is only through policies and practices of 'good governance of cultural diversity' that we will manage not only to live together in harmony, but also to turn this enforced coexistence into an opportunity for cultural and human enrichment, both at the personal and the collective level.

How can these pious wishes be transformed into concrete objectives, you will ask yourselves. Well, of course, it won't be simple, but it is feasible, provided that there is sufficient political determination and a broader participation on the part of civil society. So far, I have suggested to governments that they should draw up National Strategies for the promotion of intercultural dialogue, and that these proposals should include specific measures in the fields of education, youth, the integration of minorities and the media. And I have also proposed that they should do this not in a top-down way, but from the bottom up, or, in other words, not only through a widespread consultation of the relevant actors in civil society (NGOs, associations, foundations, the private sector, churches, etc.), but also with their participation and involvement during the implementation phase of these National Plans.

I therefore wish to make my second appeal here. And this is that each person, within the scope of their possibilities, should promote and adopt a new attitude, which, in my view, is indispensable if we wish to win this battle. A new attitude towards our fellow citizens, towards society and towards the diversity of which it is composed – both at schools and at workplaces, as well as in our neighbourhoods and buildings. A new attitude towards the sharing of the public space, in which ever more diverse groups and cultures find themselves living together. A new attitude towards our singular and collective identity, towards the values that shape it and towards the components that are intertwined within it in an open and dynamic manner. And also a new attitude towards what democracy and equal rights actually mean in terms of responsibilities and mutual respect when applied to this context of growing cultural diversity. In short, a new attitude towards the way in which we behave in our global village, where nothing is totally isolated and where the fate of humanity is at stake.

As has been suggested here by various people, albeit in different ways and sometimes with certain nuances, and reducing the idea to its bare bones, what is at stake is essentially a question of education. Education about human rights, citizenship and respect for others. Education about diversity and dialogue. Education about media literacy. Education about religions and creeds, and the possibility of dialogue between religions. We have to learn and teach intercultural skills to our citizens. We have to create urban and political strategies that will both lead to and encourage intercultural dialogue. We need policies for young people based on equal rights and equal opportunities. We need to mobilise civil society in general, young people, religious leaders and the media. We also need to broaden the agenda of the intercultural dialogue currently taking place in the context of international relations and to give it top priority.

Of course, it is not policies of intercultural dialogue that will solve problems and conflicts of a political nature, which can only be solved through the appropriate channels of negotiation. But it is also true that it is not enough just to sign treaties in order for peace to be made more lasting and sustainable: we must also create the conditions necessary for dialogue and reconciliation.

I shall end as I began, by replying to the question that has brought us together here – 'Can there be life without the Other?' – with a categorical denial: 'No', we cannot, and nor do we wish to, live without the *others* – in the plural and underlined three times. We are condemned to live with one another, if only because the other part of ourselves, left to its own devices, will exhaust itself and completely drain and empty us, as is so clearly illustrated by the solitary figure of Narcissus staring at himself in the mirror.

But we can be more ambitious and strive to make sure that the others represent, not the hell of Sartre, but rather the opportunity for the 'I' to meet the 'you', in an encounter that is a mutual celebration of differences, otherness and the diversity of ideas, opinions, values and concepts of the world and life, in which we may cultivate, as the French language puts it so beautifully, *le goût des autres*, without which, in fact, no form of cosmopolitanism makes any sense whatsoever.

28 October 2008

Translated by John Elliott

Acknowledgements

Editor
António Pinto Ribeiro

Cover design
R2 Design

Cover artwork
Yonamine

Translation
António Pinto Ribeiro, Emílio Rui Vilar, Jorge Sampaio, Manuela
Ribeiro Sanches and Ruy Duarte de Carvalho
John Elliott